DOWNTOWN GRAND MARAIS

A Brief History of the Early Hotels, the Harbor and Wisconsin Street

Eugene Glader

Previous books by author Eugene Glader:
Amateurism and Athletics
Cascade Lodge

Published by
Cascade House
1000 West 1st Street
Grand Marais, MN 55604

ISBN: 978-1-4276-4451-0

First Printing: May 2010
Printed in the USA

Cover Photo Credits
Front Cover:
Upper Left: Tourist Hotel, *Circa 1929. Courtesy of Cook County Historical Society*
Upper Right: Broadway Hotel. *Circa 1903. Courtesy of Cook County Historical Society*
Bottom: Wisconsin Street Looking East. *Circa 1917, Courtesy of Cook County Historical Society*
Back Cover:
Downtown Grand Marais. *1951. Courtesy of Cook County Historical Society.*

If you have visited Grand Marais even once, you'll be fascinated by Gene Glader's *Downtown Grand Marais – A Brief History of the Early Hotels, The Harbor and Wisconsin Street*. If you have been here many times, then you love this place – and you'll love this book. If you've never visited, *Downtown Grand Marais* is the read that will very likely change that. It's obvious from this book why Grand Marais is such an eclectic, delightfully quirky place today.

The great attention to history makes the book fascinating to read – I think I now know why our main street hugging the harbor is named Wisconsin Street! The early charts and maps show a town with streets named after past presidents, explorers, cities and states, with no apparent rationale. Photos of the earliest buildings, and the progression of locations for many of our current downtown businesses, are great fun to follow.

Read the book, and you'll feel as though you're rubbing elbows with the locals. Few towns are as fortunate as Grand Marais, to have Gene Glader relate its history with such accuracy, detail and description. Enjoy the surprises, the photos, the stories, and enjoy Grand Marais.

Diane Brostrom/Director, Grand Marais Area Tourism Association

Lucky for us, Gene Glader's passion for the story of his beloved Blue Water Café spilled beyond the corner upon which it stands. In his book "Downtown Grand Marais" Glader gives us the historical record for the ever-changing Grand Marais business district against the ever-constant backdrop of Lake Superior . After reading this book, I now look at the heart of Grand Marais through new eyes.

Sue Hakes/Mayor of Grand Marais

What an interesting book! The history of "Downtown Grand Marais" from 1873 to the present is presented with great pictures and maps. It's interesting to see the record of property ownership changes and what was built by various owners.

Alta McQuatters/President of the Cook County Historical Society

Contents

Acknowledgements

No work of this nature is possible without the help and cooperation of others. Since I began collecting information for this project many people have contributed to my effort with a word of advice, a suggestion to talk to someone, a photo or a historical fact. Among this list of people, there are at least fifty people whom I interviewed at least once during the process of gathering information for the book. Some of these people are mentioned in the endnotes of various chapters, and some are given credit for providing various photos. I want to thank all these people for their help.

There are some people and offices that I want to specifically acknowledge for their help. These are as follows: the assistance of Holly Schroeder and Dusty Nelms in the Recorder's Office in Grand Marais, the staff at the Grand Marais Public Library, the staff at the *Cook County News-Herald* newspaper, and Pat Zankman in the Cook County Historical Museum.

A special word of thanks belongs to William "Bill" Hay for his assistance in locating and interpreting property and court documents and to Kyle Oberg for helping to interpret land ownership documents and creating maps of the harbor area. I also want to acknowledge the help of Jim Ringquist in map making, editing, layout and computer assistance, and J. Reed Anderson for his editing assistance. Others who helped me with transportation and research were Bill Hennessy, Rod Wannebo, and Mike Carlson. I also want to acknowledge how helpful the book, *Pioneers In the Wilderness* by Willis "Bill" Raff has been as a reference.

A final word of appreciation belongs to my wife, Laurene, for her assistance in doing research, proof reading, and helping me with my transportation and personal needs since I became a paraplegic in August of 2007.

Eugene "Gene" Glader

Introduction

It wasn't long after purchasing the Blue Water Cafe in 1981, that I became curious about the history of the cafe and the lot on which the cafe was located. I soon discovered that a hotel was once located on the site.

After I retired I decided to research the history of the cafe and the site. Originally it was my intention that this project would comprise just a few pages relating to the cafe and the Paine Hotel that was once located on the site. Then I discovered that Mr. and Mrs. Paine, who founded the Paine Hotel, had also worked at other hotels in Grand Marais. This led to researching the history of the Mayhew, Broadway, and Grand Hotels as well as the Paine Hotel. Then it seemed appropriate to include a little history about other early hotels and boarding houses in Grand Marais.

Early in the town's history the intersection of Broadway and Wisconsin Street was the major intersection in the village, but with the development of businesses closer to the harbor the intersection at First Avenue West and Wisconsin Street became increasingly significant. Many people today would claim that the intersection where the Blue Water Cafe stands is the focal point of the town. Because it takes more than one business to create this type of focus, the businesses on the corner have always complemented each other. Consequently expanding the research on this project to include the four corners of the intersection and other nearby buildings was a very natural evolution.

By the time I had finished the research on the early hotels and the businesses on the corner of Wisconsin Street and First Avenue West it dawned on me that I had covered most of the buildings on Wisconsin Street, which runs from its intersection with Highway 61 on the west to the East Bay. By this time I had also collected several pictures and some information about the other past and present businesses on Wisconsin Street. Therefore, I decided to pursue a briefer history of the other buildings and businesses on the street. Ultimately, this became Chapter 9.

While researching the history of the various businesses I accumulated a variety of information about the early history of the town and county. All these items began to form a background for describing the history of various businesses. It also became clear that to fully understand the history of a business it was necessary to understand the cultural and historical setting in which the venture emerged. Like most towns, the emergence and growth of Grand Marais has been a complex relationship of many factors. Chapter 1 is an effort to briefly explain this setting.

Hopefully, this book will provide some interesting reading and answer some historical questions about the downtown area of Grand Marais. It is also my intent that this book will prove to be a reliable reference for others who may be interested in investigating the historical background of various lots in Grand Marais. As a minimum it is my desire that this volume will provide documentation regarding the history of a small portion of Grand Marais and Cook County.

Gene Glader
2010

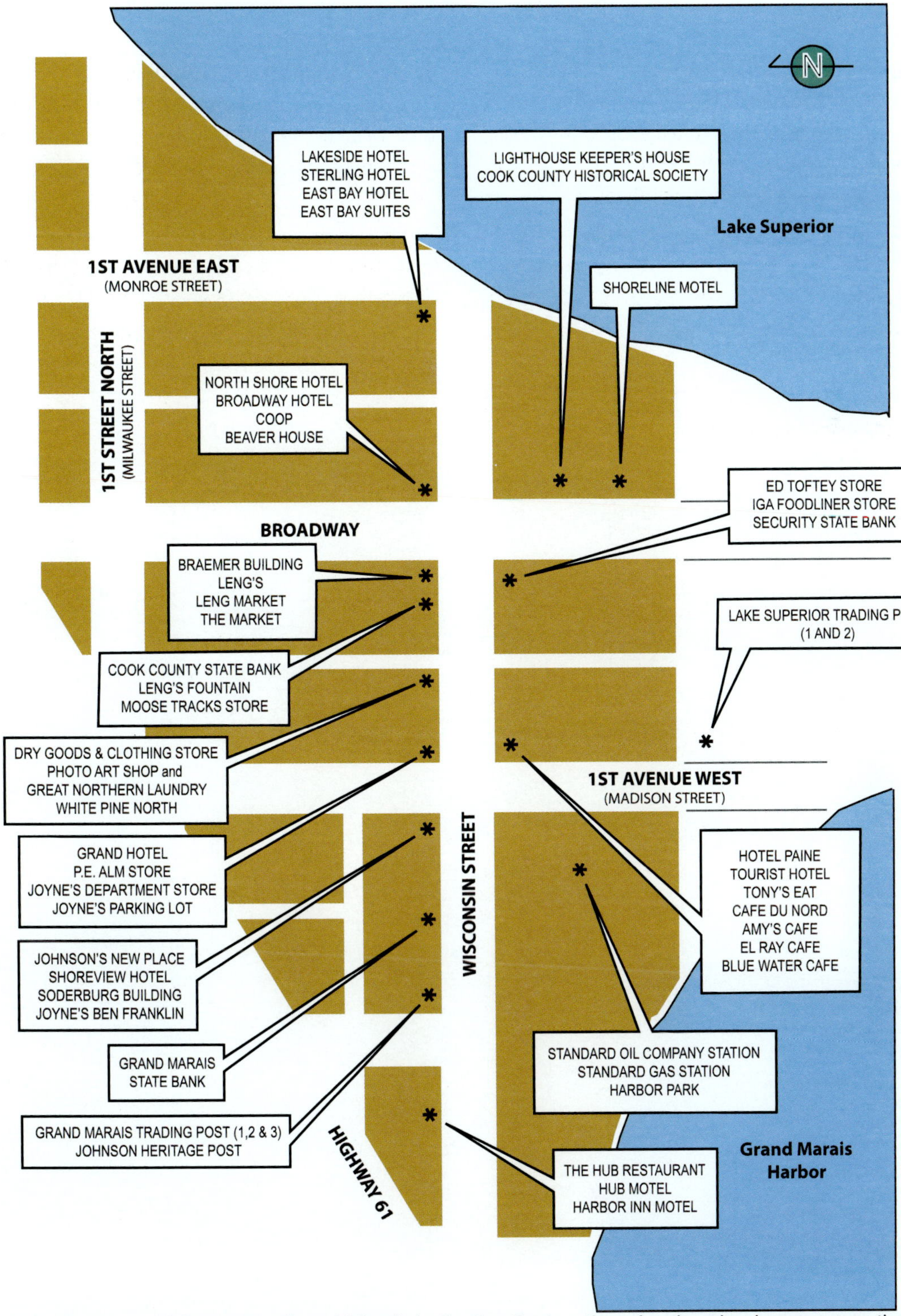

Reference map of Downtown Grand Marais indicating the location of various businesses over the last 100 years. *Map designed by Jim Ringquist.*

Chapter 1

Early History of Grand Marais

Introduction

Obtaining an understanding of the setting in which a business or organization emerged is helpful while studying the history of any enterprise. So it was for me as I researched the history of the Blue Water Cafe site and the history of the early hotels and lots located near the cafe. Questions such as the following began to surface: (1) What prompted these businesses to develop? (2) What was attracting people to the area at the time the businesses emerged? and (3) What was it like to live in Cook County during the pioneer days?

Consequently, as this book began to take shape it became apparent that a brief review of the history of the Grand Marais area would be helpful to readers. Thus, this chapter was written in an effort to provide a brief historical background to the emergence of some of the early hotels, restaurants, and businesses in Grand Marais.

The need for lodging facilities in Grand Marais probably began shortly after the signing of the Treaty of LaPointe between the U.S. Government and seven chiefs of the Chippewa Indian Peace Commission in September of 1854. This document opened up all of Cook, Lake, and Carleton counties, and some other areas, for white settlement. According to Willis Raff, the author of *Pioneers in the Wilderness*, "The signing of this Treaty opened up the floodgates to many mineral entrepreneurs and prospectors who were then finally able to act upon their hopes and dreams..."[1] The fact that Minnesota didn't become a state until 1858 helps illustrate the undeveloped status of the territory in the mid-1800's when this treaty was signed.

During the early research for this book I thought that a chronology of ownership back to the person who purchased various lots from the U. S. Government would be interesting and helpful information for the reader. It soon became apparent that such detail, prior to about 1900, for most properties would detract from the purpose of the book. Therefore, the entire chronology of ownership for all parcels written about in this volume is not always included.

Early Land Owners

Two of the early purchasers of land in the downtown area of what would become Grand Marais were Robert Humes and John Butler. For example, the first entry in the Abstract of the Blue Water Cafe property is for a patent (Ownership Documents) given to Robert Humes on November 30, 1872, for a large portion of land in what was to become Grand Marais. The second entry is for the conveyance of this land to William Stretch with a Warranty Deed on October 4, 1871. Apparently Robert Humes had claimed and applied for a patent on the land from the United States Government, but did not receive the actual patent until November 30, 1872.[2]

Another early purchaser of three, eighty acre parcels of land that would become part of Grand Marais was John Butler. In May and June of 1873, he received patents from the United States Government for these parcels.[3] These land speculators soon sold parts or all of these parcels of land to others.

Among the early entrepreneurs and prospectors that came to live in Cook County were Samuel F. Howenstine, Henry Mayhew and Ted Wakelin. By 1870, these three men had established themselves in Grand Marais and by 1873 had "... secured all the land comprising the original village [Grand Marais] and the lands facing the Lake on the West Bay, as well as the East Bay."[4] An additional quote from Willis Raff helps explain their incentive in owning this land:

> Throughout the remainder of the century, they carefully retained control of those valuable properties by means of a confusing tangle of partnerships, court actions, and interlocking corporate directorships for the building of general-purpose docks, warehouses, railroad right-of-ways, and ore docks.[5]

In March 1874, the Minnesota Legislature established Cook County as a separate governmental unit. Prior to that time Cook County was part of Lake County. However, the local government of Cook County did not begin to function until September 7, 1882, when the governor appointed the first county commissioners.[6] The Town [Township] of Grand Marais was formally organized in August of 1899.

The ownership of land in the Town of Grand Marais began to change in 1887, when Edward W. Wakelin sold significant portions of land to Mr. and Mrs. John H. Walcott who in turn sold it to the Grand Marais Real Estate and Improvement Company.[7] This company was incorporated in Wisconsin on April 16, 1887, and made its headquarters in Milwaukee, Wisconsin.[8] Most, if not all, of the investors in this company were from the Milwaukee and Chicago areas. The company then hired Gustave Steinhagen to survey and plat much of this land into lots, blocks, streets and alleys. This task was completed and filed with the county on June 27, 1887. The filed document states that the platted map of the land the corporation owned in the village was a "free act and deed of said corporation."[9] The term "village" is used for Grand Marais in this document, but the town was not incorporated as a village until

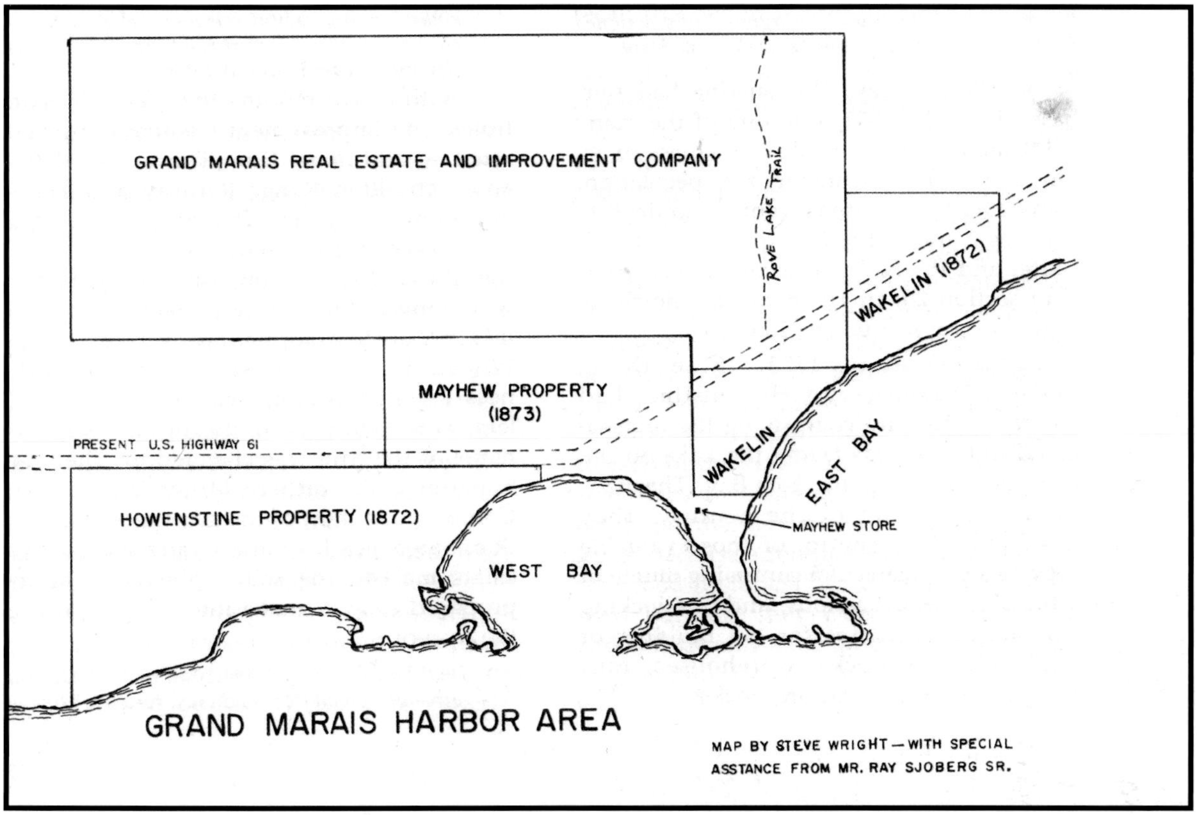

The above map is from the book *Pioneers in the Wilderness*, by Willis Raff, p. 18. The map was made by Steve Wright with special assistance from Mr. Ray Sjoberg Sr. in the late 1970's or early 1980's. The land in the above map, which indicates ownership by Wakelin, was included in the land surveyed and platted by the Grand Marais Real Estate and Improvement Company in 1887. The Grand Marais Real Estate and Improvement Company claimed ownership of most if not all of Wakelin's land in the above map on June 27, 1887.

February 1903.[10]

As part of the compensation for the above land transactions, Samuel L. Bayless was given twelve newly platted lots, and Edward W. Wakelin twenty-eight newly platted lots scattered among several blocks in Grand Marais.[11] The sale of land from Wakelin to Walcott to the Grand Marais Real Estate and Improvement Company all took place on April 27, 1887, and was filed in the Court House on July 6, 1887. The transfer of these parcels from Wakelin, to John H. Walcott, to the Grand Marais Real Estate and Improvement Company on the same day raises the question of the role of Walcott in the transactions. Was he a clever, independent businessman who put these transactions together; or was he hired as an intermediary by the Grand Marais Real Estate and Improvement Company to create a series of transactions that ended with the Grand Marais Real Estate and Improvement Company owning a very large portion of the emerging Village of Grand Marais?

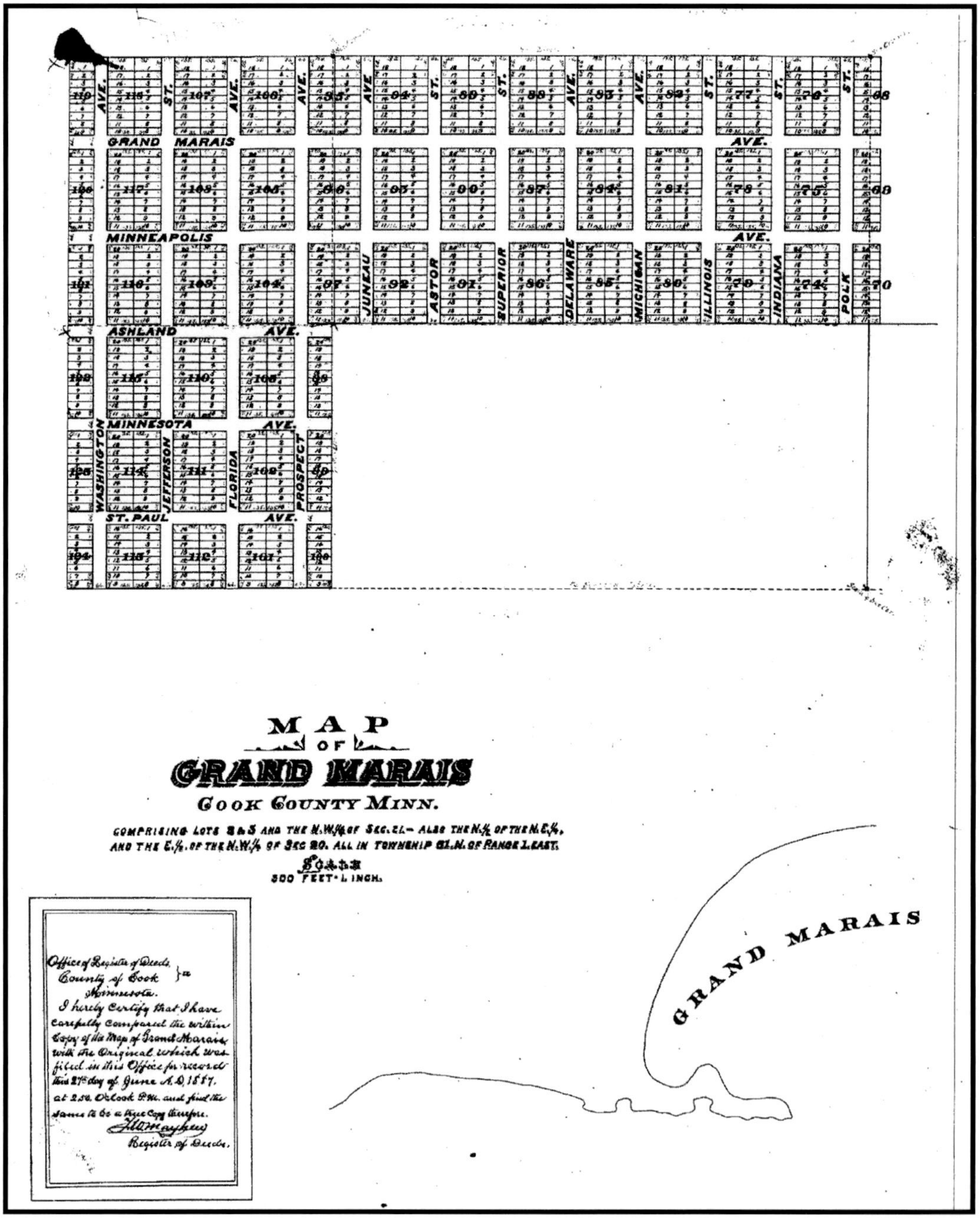

The Western part of the Village Plat Map made by Gustave Steinhagen for the Grand Marais Real Estate and Improvement Company. The Grand Marais Real Estate and Improvement Company claimed it owned all the platted land in the map when the officers of the company gave it to the Village of Grand Marais in June 27, 1887. *(The map is courtesy of the Cook County Court House Recorders Office.)*

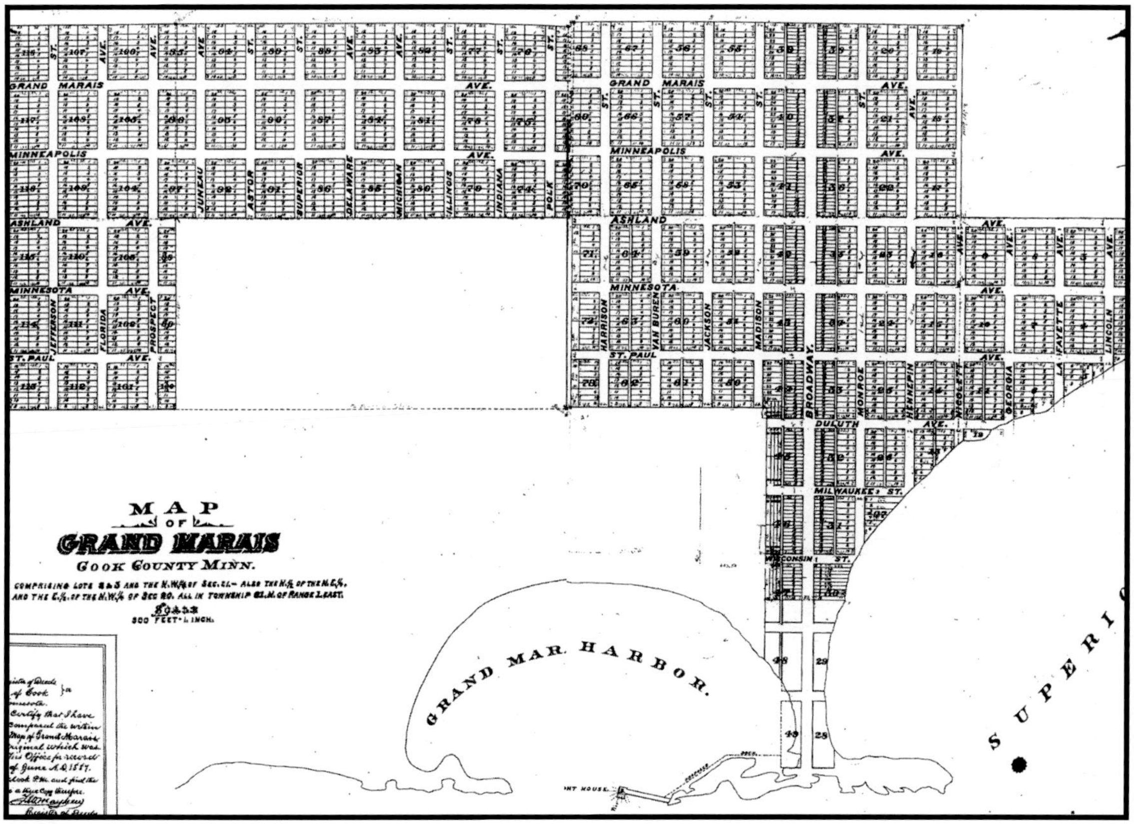

This is a map of the Eastern part of the Village Plat Map made by Gustave Steinhagen for the Grand Marais Real Estate and Improvement Company. The Grand Marais Real Estate and Improvement Company claimed it owned all the platted land in the map when the officers of the company gave it to the Village of Grand Marais in June 27, 1887. *(The map is courtesy of the Cook County Court House Recorders Office.)*

Included in the Plat Map of the Village of Grand Marais given to the county in 1887, was the naming of all the streets and avenues in the Village. The list of names included a seemingly random selection of cities, states, past U.S. Presidents, and early explorers. There was also an avenue named Prospect, and the name Broadway for the main road to the Point where Mayhew's home and business was located. There was no apparent order or rationale for the names of the streets and avenues. That is most likely the reason why the Village Council of Grand Marais passed a resolution on August 2, 1927, renaming all the streets and avenues, except Wisconsin Street and Broadway.[12] There never was a street called Main Street. However, Broadway was the main street for many years, and in many respects Wisconsin became the main street perhaps as early as 1920.

The Grand Marais Real Estate and Improvement Company advertised its lots with advertisements of various sizes and designs virtually every week between 1891 and 1920. May 30, 1891, marked the beginning of the first local newspaper, the *Pioneer,*

Advertisement in *Cook County Herald,* June 24, 1905. This advertisement was approximately a one-quarter page in size and ran for months.

in Grand Marais. It was published by A. DeLacy Wood and sold to Chris Murphy in June of 1893. Chris Murphy then promptly changed the name of the paper to the *Cook County Herald.*[13]

Major Changes in Ownership of Harbor Land

The ownership of the land around the Grand Marais Harbor began a dramatic shift in 1900, when Charles J. Johnson purchased a significant portion of land on the west side of the harbor from Samuel Howenstine.[14] (Refer to map on Page 8.) On September 8, 1903, an even bigger and more significant transaction took place when Charles J. Johnson purchased from Mr. & Mrs. Hazael Mayhew an undivided three-quarters interest in land basically consisting of the current site of the Harbor Park and the lots comprising the Blue Water Cafe site and approximately the front twenty-five feet of the Lake Superior Trading Post property and an entire interest in all of the land south of the current trading post and a small slice of land on the west side of the harbor on Lake Superior.[15] The purchase included land on which the current Coast Guard Station is located and land today known as "Artist Point," and land jutting out toward the harbor entrance. Mayhew's store, hotel and other buildings on the "Point" were also included in the purchase. The price for this transaction was $25,000. These purchases gave Charles J. Johnson almost complete ownership of the land around the Grand Marais Harbor. The exception was a 700-foot wide parcel on the west side of the harbor that Samuel Howenstine sold to Cuyler Adams and William White on January 23, 1903.[16 i]

On April 4, 1904, Charles J. Johnson transferred all of his property mentioned in items numbered 1 through 5 (on the map on page 8) to the Grand Marais Dock Company, a Minnesota corporation in which he was a principal investor.[17]

After the transfer of Charlie Johnson's interests in the above properties to the Grand Marais Dock Company, a dispute developed over the ownership of the land in which the Grand Marais Dock Company claimed three-fourth ownership, This resulted in the Grand Marais Dock Company filing a claim in court against John Paulson, and the more than twenty-five people and organizations, disputing the company's ownership. To solve the dispute a district court judge on May 4, 1905, appointed D. B. McAlpine, as a referee, to conduct a public auction to sell the disputed parcels separately to the highest bidder. The auction was held on July 18, 1905.[18]

The Grand Marais Realty Company, which was formed as a corporation, as recently as March 1905,[19] was the highest bidder for the three parcels. The Grand Marais Realty Company, of which Charlie Johnson was the president and principal owner, bid a total of $18,000 for the three parcels of land in question. These parcels included what today are basically the current Harbor Park [i] and the Blue Water Cafe lot and the front half of the Lake Superior Trading Post property. On September 7, 1905, the court officially gave the ownership of the property to the Grand Marais Realty Company.[20]

Population Growth and Shipping

Following the early mineral prospectors who came to Cook County, were the lumber companies and the large crews for harvesting the timber, especially during the period of 1890 to 1920. Another category of people

[i] Mr. & Mrs. William White sold their interest in the parcel to Cuyler Adams on September 22, 1910. [Book G, Quit Claim Deeds Record, p. 340, Recorders Office, Cook County Court House, Grand Marais, Minnesota]. November 11, 1925, Adams sold the parcel to George Leng. [Book Z, Quit Claim Deeds Record, p. 151, Recorders Office, Cook County Court House, Grand Marais, Minnesota].

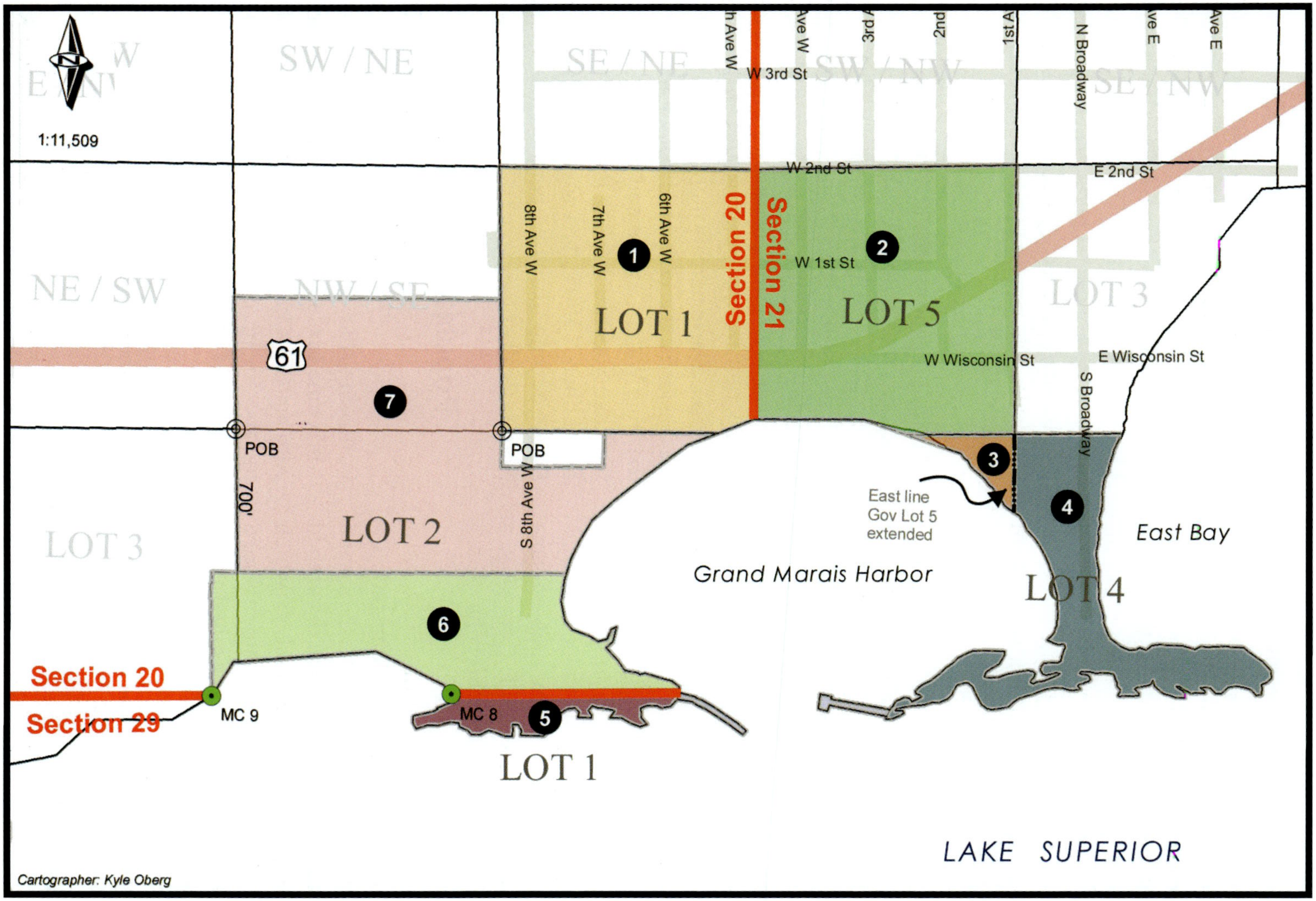

Grand Marais Harbor and Lands owned by Charles Johnson, Cuyler Adams and William White.
(Map courtesy of Kyle Oberg, Cartographer.)

< Legend for Map (Opposite Page):

Property Purchased by Charles J. Johnson from Mr. & Mrs. Hazael Mayhew on September 8, 1903 for $25,000.00:

#1. Undivided three-fourth of Government lot 1, Section 20.
#2. Undivided three-fourth of Government lot 5, Section 21.
#3. Undivided three-fourth of that part of Government lot 4 in Section 21, which lies between the Grand Marais Harbor and the east line of Government lot 5, extending to the shore of said harbor.
#4. The entire interest in all of Government lot 4, Section 21.
#5. All of Government lot 1 in Section 29, Township 61, North of Range 1.

Property Purchased from Mr. and Mrs. Samuel Howenstine:

#6 Parcel purchased by Charles J. Johnson on September 8, 1903.
#7 Parcel purchased by Cuyler Adams and Mr. and Mrs. William White on January 23, 1903.

Property Purchased at auction from the Grand Marais Realty Company on September 7, 1905

#1, Government lot 1, in Section 20 sold for $7,000.00.
#2, Government lot 5 in Section 21 sold for $9,000.00.
#3, that part of Government lot 4 in Section 21, which lies between the Grand Marais Harbor and the east line of Government lot 5, extending to the shore of said harbor sold for $2,000.00

who came to Cook County during this period was the homesteaders. The homesteaders were primarily immigrants who came to take up fishing, farming, and working in the woods for a livelihood. The combination of lumbering interests, mineral interests and immigrants brought about significant transportation developments in and around Grand Marais between 1880 and 1920.

From 1910 to 2000 the residents of Grand Marais made up an average of 30.74 percent of the county's total population. The percentage of people living in Grand Marais increased to an average of almost 35 percent for the years 1910 to 2000 if you: (1) assume that the number of people living within one-half mile of the city boundary equals ten percent of the number of people living within the city boundary and (2) count them in the city population,

The use of ships on Lake Superior for personal travel and commercial purposes was the first major transportation development. It is noteworthy that by 1883 the Booth

Population of Grand Marais and Cook County[ii]

Year	Grand Marais	Cook County	% of Population Living in Grand Marais
1880	Not Available	65	Not Available
1890	Not Available	95	Not Available
1900	Not Available	810	Not Available
1910	355	1336	19.09%
1920	443	1841	24.46
1930	618	2435	25.38
1940	855	3030	28.22
1950	1078	2900	37.17
1960	1301[iii]	3377	38.53
1970	1301	3423	38.01
1980	1289	4092	31.5
1990	1171	3868	30.27
2000	1353	5168	26.18

[ii] It is probable that the census figures before 1924 do not include all the Native Americans in the county, because Native Americans were not citizens until 1924. The law at the time stated that unless individual Indians paid taxes they were not to be counted in calculating the population figures for congressional representation. In 1924 Congress passed a law making all Indians U. S. citizens. The non-citizen status of Indians prior to 1924 is related to the fact that the U. S. Government recognized Indian tribes as sovereign governments from the very beginning of the existence of the U.S. Government. *[Internet site:lawlib.lclark.edu/blog/native_america/?page_id=10, Robert J. Miller, American Indians and the United States Constitution.]*

[iii] Data for years 1900 through 2000 comes from U.S. Census Bureau web site. The identical figures for the Grand Marais population in 1960 and 1970 are correct.

Fishing Company began running boats to Grand Marais on a regular schedule. By the turn of the century several different ships stopped regularly in Grand Marais and by May 1902, the America was stopping three times a week during the shipping season.[22] The steamer America was a well known, first class passenger and freight ship that traversed a regular route for twenty-six years from Duluth to Isle Royale to Port Arthur, Ontario, with many stops along the way. The ship's unexpected end came on June 7, 1928, when it struck a reef and sank at Isle Royale[iv]. During this period the local newspaper listed the names of people coming and going on ships or other means of transportation in almost every issue.

Stages, Roads and Railroads

Another mode of transportation that emerged involved improvements in roads and trails. In this regard, a major improvement in travel between Duluth and Grand Marais came with the completion of the new bridge over the Cascade River and the construction of the final segments of the Lake Shore Road in Lake and Cook Counties in 1899. The first stage coach using the new road arrived in Grand Marais on December 19, 1899.[23]

The third major form of transportation that emerged, mainly due to lumbering and mining interests was the railroad. Between 1898 and 1928, a large railroad network was developed from Duluth to Clearwater Lake to support logging. Due to the discovery of iron ore in the area of Gunflint Lake, a railroad was built during 1891 and 1892 from Port Arthur, Canada, to the Paulson mine near Gunflint Lake. The railroad was called the Port Arthur, Duluth and Western Railway (PAD&W). By the end of 1893, the Paulson mine had failed and the rail connection between the western end of Cook County and Port Arthur began to decline and was last used in about 1904. From 1890 to 1915, there were several efforts and various plans developed to connect Grand Marais by rail to Port Arthur and Duluth. One effort to build a railroad into Grand Marais was for the purpose of hauling logs to the harbor. The plans for this railroad were reported in 1904 as follows:

> The Nestor company is making active preparations for its logging operations in Cook County, which will be conducted on a large scale this winter. According to current rumors these preparations are to include the construction of ten miles of railway extending from Grand Marais into the company's timber holdings near Devils Track Lake. Wednesday night a crew of forty men arrived in charge of a foreman, and these have been put to work building a camp, which is to be located about five miles from town, and making all necessary preliminary arrangements for a much larger force to come in a few days. We are informed that the company will put 300 men at [sic] work on the road within a very short time and will

[iv] As a new boat, the America was operated as an excursion boat between Buffalo, N.Y. and Niagara Falls for two seasons prior to being purchased by the Booth Company in early 1902.

Wagon Road Bridge over the Cascade River built in 1899. *Circa 1910.*

have it completed and equipped before the logging season opens. A tug came in Thursday with a barge loaded with lumber, tools and supplies.[25]

The Nestor Company plans and other plans for a railroad into Grand Marais never came to fruition. The consequence of these failures to build a railroad into Grand Marais is the fact that the harbor area was protected from major industrial development and was preserved to become the beautiful setting it is today. For the interested reader a summary of the efforts to build a railroad to Grand Marais is well documented in the books *Pioneers in the Wilderness*, and *Minnesota Logging Railroads*.

The possibility of building a railroad to or from the harbor of Grand Marais made the land around the harbor prime land for investors. From 1873, when Wakelin, Howenstine, and Mayhew owned all the land around the harbor, the land changed hands many times as individuals and corporations purchased various parcels. During the years from 1873 to about 1905, the abstracts of various lots around the harbor reveal complex records of investors and speculators purchasing and selling parcels of land and fractional interests in parcels of land. Sometimes a person or corporation may have had as small an investment as a one-sixty-fourth interest in a parcel of land. Much of this investment speculation was driven by the possibility of a railroad, warehouses and docks being built near or on the harbor.

The Village of Grand Marais Grows

The combined impact of lumbering, mining, farming, fishing, the emergence of county and village governmental entities, and transportation needs created many jobs in the area. Some of the jobs included in this mix were prospectors, investors, managers, supervisors, surveyors, geologists and hundreds of laborers. This large mix of people created the need for a variety of other businesses and organizations such as construction companies, retail stores, barber shops, livery stables, restaurants, hotels, churches and a local newspaper.

An additional sign of progress in the village was the installation of a telephone in the courthouse in 1902 as part of a small local telephone system.[26] In August of the same year, a new telephone company was organized to build a telephone line between Two Harbors and Grand Marais. A telephone line already existed between Duluth and Two Harbors. The article reporting this development explained the need for such a telephone line as follows:

> The need of a telephone system between Grand Marais and this city [Duluth] has been talked of for some time, and the residents of that thriving town have looked upon it as a necessity. In the winter the people are left wholly without communication with the outside world. This begins when the last boat leaves in the fall, and continues until the first one arrives in the spring. The mail [in the winter] is carried by [dog] team to Two Harbors, and in case of an emergency the people have been without any method by which a hurried word could be sent.[27]

As the population of the county grew churches also were established. The first denomination to build a church in Grand Marais was the Catholic Church which built its first church in 1897. The next church to be organized was the Norwegian Lutheran Church in 1892, and they built their first church in 1898. In 1907, the Congregational Church became the third denomination to organize a church,[28] followed by the organization of the Baptist Church in 1924.

Another sign of growth shortly after the turn of the century was the building of sidewalks in the village of Grand Marais. On October 5, 1903, the Village Council authorized the construction of a sidewalk on the north side of Wisconsin Street from the southwest corner of block 46 [First Avenue West] to the east side of Broadway Street.[29] The sidewalk was "To be built eight feet wide, the material to be used to be [sic] pine, spruce or tamarack planks, two inches thick, surface on top side, to be laid on three stringers not less than 4 by 4 inches, said stringers to be laid on cedar blocks or post in the usual manner of laying sidewalks..."[30] At this same meeting the Village Council also approved construction of a sidewalk on the west side of Monroe Street [First Avenue East] from the south side of Milwaukee Street [First Street] to St. Paul Street [Third Street].

In the fall of 1904, the Village Council had twelve streetlights installed along the principal streets in the village.[31] These lamps burned some type of fuel and had to be lit each night.

In October 1904, the Village Council authorized the construction of an additional sidewalk in Grand Marais.

> The sidewalk also was to be six feet wide and built of pine, spruce or tamarack planks two inches thick, laid on stringers not less than 4 x 4 inches. The sidewalk was to be on the north side of St. Paul Street [today's Third

A baseball game on the Grand Marais Harbor. Note the Sidewalk or Boardwalk. It appears that the end of the above sidewalk is the one built in 1903 on the north side of Wisconsin Street starting at First Avenue West to Broadway. The ball field appears to be located where the Harbor Park is currently located. *Circa 1903-1909. (Photo Courtesy of Cook County Historical Society.)*

> Street], from the west side of Monroe Street [First Avenue East] to the southeast corner of block 72, along the west side of Harrison Street [Fourth Avenue West] to the southeast corner of block 73 [the block where the current Court House sits].[32]

In 1921, the Village began converting the wooden sidewalks to concrete sidewalks.[33] This also marked the year that an electric light (generating) plant began operating in Grand Marais.[34]

Beginning around 1891, the harbor was enlarged when gravel was dredged from the harbor for the building of streets in Duluth and Superior. This, plus wind and waves over the years, expanded the harbor to the north, reducing the area where baseball was played.[35] The hauling of gravel from the harbor and the East Bay went on for many years. As late as 1932, the Chief Engineer of the Corps of Engineers of the U.S. Army in Washington D.C., had recommended to the Secretary of War, who had forwarded to Congress a recommendation that the Grand Marais Harbor be enlarged about 450 feet in a westerly direction and deepened to 20 feet in the vicinity of the entrance. The local newspaper report of this recommendation explained the need for this improvement as follows:

> These improvements are designed to afford safer entry into and better protection to shipping within the harbor. This harbor is used as a base for vessels belonging to the fishing fleet and as a harbor of refuge for small craft generally along the North Shore. At present it is the only reasonably safe harbor between Agate Bay (Two Harbors), and the international border, a distance of 126 miles. These improvements involve the excavation of about 99,000 yards of material from the harbor basin and the placing of about 800 cubic yards of concrete. It is estimated that the total cost of this work will be in the neighborhood of $44,000 reports say.
>
> Since these improvements, especially the construction of a sea wall will benefit local dock owners, the District Engineer has recommended the improvement be made conditional upon the conveyance to the United States, free of all costs, of all necessary right-of-way and easements over the land on which the sea wall is to be constructed.[36]

The above recommendations were completed in 1937 by building a breakwater at the entrance of the harbor and construction of a sea wall across the ledge at the southeast corner of the harbor and dredging of 36.5 acres of the harbor to a depth of 16 to 20 feet.[37]

By 1904, the Village Council was giving serious consideration to filling in what was called the "pond" where the current municipal parking lot and a portion of Broadway is located. There were economic and sanitary reasons for wanting to fill in the pond. The pond covered an area of about twenty lots and part of Broadway. "According to the engineer's report the depth of the pond is from three to five feet, and the bottom is a mass of mire and filth. Especially during hot weather there is a constant stench that at times is unbearable."[38]

After efforts to receive bids for the project failed, the Village Council decided in the fall of 1905 to take on the project themselves with hired day workers and a person to superintend the job.[39] Opening up Broadway to what is now Highway 61 was a significant asset to the businesses south of the "pond." It certainly contributed to making Broadway and Wisconsin Street the focal point of the Village for many years.

Improvements in Roads

There were two periods in which major highway improvement between Duluth and Grand Marais and Thunder Bay, Ontario, took place. The first was in 1917, when the new automobile road, Highway 1, was completed between Duluth and Port Arthur, Ontario.[40][v] Highway 1 was just a gravel road at this time, but it opened Grand Marais to automobile and truck traffic. By November 1919, a Canadian immigration and customs officer reported that 1,930 cars and over

[v] Port Arthur and Fort William were merged and renamed Thunder Bay in 1970.

10,000 people had traveled to and from Canada over the North Shore road during the previous tourist season. It was also estimated that another 10,000 Canadian and/or American tourists traveled to the border and back during the same time period.[41]

The second major improvement in Highway 1 came during the early 1930's. The State of Minnesota Commissioner of Highways ordered the new design for Highway 1 in Cook County and through Grand Marais in August 1930.[42] The original route of Highway 1 is the current route of County Road 7. During the next few months and years the right-of-way for the new highway was purchased and the highway was built.

By the fall of 1934, a totally new and black-topped highway was finished from Duluth to Grand Marais. This was a significant boost to the economy of Grand Marais and Cook County. Highway 1 was renumbered in 1934 and became Highway 61.

A Municipal Water and Sewage Systems

In 1933, and perhaps earlier, discussions were held regarding the needs for a municipal water and sewage system in Grand Marais. In an announcement calling for a mass meeting to discuss the issues the following paragraphs stated the concerns of many.

> There is no question but what a water works system in Grand Marais would go a long way toward lowering the fire insurance rates in the village. These rates at the present time are almost prohibitive, due to the lack of proper fire protection, which a water works system would supply. A public system of sewage disposal is a crying need in the village, and as the years go by the need of one will eventually be an absolute necessity. When it is considered that there are a number of private cess pools here, which drain into the ground, filtering down hill, making the central part of the business section its final accumulating point, there can be no question but that in time this part will become a breeding point for disease and epidemics. Water is being pumped out of the ground here which, if it is not now, will in time become contaminated and dangerous for use as drinking water.[43]

This meeting kicked off a process to proceed with efforts to build a new water system. These efforts included applying for and receiving a significant grant from the Public Works Administration [PWA], a federal agency, for the system.[44] It wasn't until April 1936, that Grand Marais was able to celebrate the addition of a municipal water system.[45] The water for the system came from five springs on Maple Hill flowing through pipes by force of gravity, consequently requiring no pumping stations to maintain good water pressure at all times.[46] In a year-end summary of improvements in the Village the local newspaper reported, "The newly acquired water works almost requires a sewer system to care for the sewage disposal. Although plans were approved, no money was yet available for that project."[47]

A municipal sewer system was installed in the Village in 1938. It is hard to imagine Grand Marais with perhaps fifty to one-hundred private water sources and septic systems or out houses prior to 1937. Other projects that were completed in the Village in 1937 were (1) a seawall was constructed to hold back the lake from encroaching on Highway 61; (2) light standards were put up by the Village along Highway 61 into town, creating what was locally called the first "great white way" for the town; (3) downtown streets received a coat of tar, and curbs were constructed on the main business streets, (4) 7,710 feet of concrete sidewalks were built with labor from the Works Progress Administration [WPA] crews; and (5) the Gateway entrance to the Gunflint Trail was begun by Civilian Conservation Corps crews [CCC].[48]

The information in the preceding pages was included to briefly explain the setting in which early hotels and restaurants emerged. Hopefully the above facts will make the following chapters more enjoyable and meaningful.

(Endnotes)

1. Willis H. Raff, *Pioneers in the Wilderness* (Grand Marais, MN: Cook County Historical Society, 1981), p.4.

2. Book B. Transcribed Records of Lake County, Minnesota, page 63.

3. Blue Water Cafe Abstract, entries 12, 13, and 14.

4. Willis H. Raff, *Pioneers in the Wilderness* (Grand Marais, MN: Cook County Historical Society, 1981), p.17.

5. Willis H. Raff, *Pioneers in the Wilderness* (Grand Marais, MN: Cook County Historical Society, 1981), p.17.

6. F. B. Hicks, "Historian Tells of Early Beginnings of Grand Marais as an Indian Trading Post," *Duluth News Tribune*, October 6, 1929, p. 12.

7. Book A, Deed Records, pp. 248, 249, 250, 258, 259 and 260. Recorders Office, Cook County Court House, Grand Marais, MN

8. Willis H. Raff, *Pioneers in the Wilderness* (Grand Marais, MN: Cook County Historical Society, 1981), p.17.

9. Map of Village of Grand Marais, filed in Cook County Court House, June 27, 1887.

10. "Petition and Notice of Election," *Cook County Herald*, March 7, 1903, p. 3

11. Book B, Warranty Deed Record, pp. 2 and 5, Recorders Office, Cook County Court House, Grand Marais, Minnesota.

12. Resolution, Grand Marais Village Council, Grand Marais, MN, August 2, 1927.

13. Willis H. Raff, *Pioneers in the Wilderness* (Grand Marais, MN: Cook County Historical Society, 1981), pp.66&-67.

14. Book F, Warranty Deed Record, p. 211, Recorders Office, Cook County Court House, Grand Marais, Minnesota.

15. Book I, Warranty Deed Recorded, p. 186, Recorders Office, Cook County Court House, Grand Marais, Minnesota.

16. ,Book 1, Deed Record, p. 116, Recorders Office, Cook County Court House, Grand Marais, Minnesota.

17. Book K, Warranty Deed Record, p. 417, Recorders Office, Cook County Court House, Grand Marais, MN.

18. Book O, Deed Record, p. 185, Recorders Office, Cook County Court House, Grand Marais, MN.

19. "Articles of Incorporation of the Grand Marais Realty Company, *Cook County Herald,* April 15, 1905, P. 7.

20. Book O, Deed Record, p. 185, Recorders Office, Cook County Court House, Grand Marais, Minnesota.

21. F. B. Hicks, "Historian Tells of Early Beginnings of Grand Marais as an Indian Trading Post," *Duluth News Tribune*, October 6, 1929, p. 12.

22. "Caught on the Run," *Cook County Herald*, May 17, 1902, p. 5

23. "Happenings" *Cook County Herald*, December 23, 1899, p. 3.

24. Frank A. King, Minnesota Logging Railroads (San Marino, California: Golden West Books, 1981), Insert between pp. 50 and 51.

25. "THE NESTOR COMPANY," *Cook County Herald*, September 24, 1904, p. 5.

26."Caught on the Run," *Cook County Herald*, June 28, 1902, p. 5

27. "THE TELEPHONE COMPANY," *Cook County Herald*, August 9, 1902, p. 5

28. F. B. Hicks, "Historian Tells of Early Beginnings of Grand Marais as an Indian Trading Post," *Duluth News Tribune*, October 6, 1929, p. 12.

29. "RESOLUTION," *Cook County Herald*, November 12, 1904, p. 4.

30. "VILLAGE COUNCIL PROCEEDINOS [sic]," *Cook County Herald*, November, 1903, p. 5.

30. Ibid. "VILLAGE COUNCIL PROCEEDINOS [sic]," *Cook County Herald*, November, 1903, p. 5.

31. "LOCAL ITEMS," *Cook County Herald*, October 8, 1904, p. 5.

32. "RESOLUTION," *Cook County Herald*, October 15, 1904, p. 4.

33. "Bids for Sidewalk," *Cook County Herald*, April 28, 1921, p. 3.

34. "Grand Marais Getting Ready for Electric Plant," Cook *County News-Herald*, December 9, 1920, p. 1.

35. Willis H. Raff, *Pioneers in the Wilderness* (Grand Marais, MN: Cook County Historical Society, 1981), pp. 63-64.

36. Harbor Improvements Approved," Cook *County News-Herald*, May 10, 1932, p. 1.

37. "New Developments In Harbor Issue," *Cook County Herald*, April 14, 1938, p.1.

38. "PLANS TO FILL THE POND," *Cook County Herald*, February 6, 1904, p. 7.

39. "Broadway Improvement," *Cook County Herald*, October 7, 1905, p. 5.

40. "The Formal Opening of the Duluth-Port Arthur Highway to be Celebrated by Proper Ceremonies," Cook *County News-Herald*, August 15, 1917, p. 1.

41. "OVER TWENTY THOUSAND TOURISTS OVER SHORE ROAD," Cook *County News-Herald*, November 26, 1919, p. 1.

42. Book 5, Miscellaneous Records, pp. 425 & 426, Recorders Office, Cook County Court House, Grand Marais, Minnesota.

43. "Mass Meeting Called to Discuss Water System and Sewage Disposal," Cook *County News-Herald*, September 7, 1933, p. 1.

44. "Day Proclaimed Holiday For Water Celebration," Cook *County News-Herald*, April 23, 1936, p. 1.

45. "Banquet; Celebration To Start New System," Cook *County News-Herald*, April 16, 1936, p. 1.

46. "Ample Water Supply Assured By Location of Five Springs," Cook *County News-Herald*, August 1, 1935, p. 4.

47. "Many Improvements In Village This Year," Cook *County News-Herald*, December 23, 1937, p. 1.

48. "Many Improvements In Village This Year," Cook *County News-Herald*, December 23, 1937, p. 1.

Chapter 2

Brief History of the Blue Water Cafe Site

Connection of Blue Water Site to West Side of Harbor

The history of the site of the Blue Water Cafe has an interesting connection to the Cook County Manufacturing Company sawmill which was built on the west side of the harbor on land that Charles Johnson had purchased from Samuel Howenstine in 1900. Construction of the mill began in April 1904, and the sawing of lumber began in August 1904. Mr. D. Cowie of Bayfield, Wisconsin was president of the company and Samuel Bally of Bayfield and Charles J. Johnson of Grand Marais were two of the other principal investors in the company.[1]

By the summer of 1905, the expansion of the mill required the employment of fifty men. Many of the men had difficulty finding room and board in Grand Marais, so the company, or Charles Johnson personally, built a two-story frame boarding house for the men on the west side of the harbor near the sawmill.[2] The building had fifteen rooms and was ready for occupancy by July 1905.[3]

The mill was producing lumber at least

Picture and subtitle from *Cook County Herald*, July 22, 1905, p. 6. The building at the right is the sawmill boarding house. The sub-title reads as follows: The Cook County Manufacturing Company Sawmill and Boarding House. *(From a sketch drawn by Geo. H. Durfee.)*

through 1907, but that appears to have been the last year of operation due in part to major losses of logs being rafted to Grand Marais on Lake Superior during storms.[4] Consequently, the need for a boarding house near the sawmill site came to an end.

From pictures and drawings of the sawmill and boarding house it appears that the operation was at least partially on a 700-foot wide parcel of land owned by Cuyler Adams and Mr. and Mrs. William White. If the sawmill operation was not on their land, people at least had to cross their land to get to the mill. Perhaps Cuyler Adams and the Whites were investors in the Cook County Manufacturing Company or perhaps they rented or leased the land to the corporation for a few years. We just don't know.

We do know that Mr. Adams and Mr. and Mrs. White purchased the parcel from Mr. and Mrs. Samuel Howenstine in January 1903.[5] Then on September 22, 1910, the Whites sold their interest in the parcel to Cuyler Adams.[6] Some years later on November 11, 1925, Mr. Adams sold the parcel to Mr. and Mrs. George (Ella) Leng.[7] Ella Leng was a sister to Charlie Johnson. Eventually the land became part of the Grand Marais Tourist Park.

The Hotel Paine Emerges

This leads to the connection of the sawmill on west side of the Grand Marais Harbor with the site of the Blue Water Cafe. In December of 1908, Fred Paine had returned to Grand Marais for the purpose of going into the hotel business. Several factors came together to bring Mr. and Mrs. Paine back from Canada to open up their own hotel in Grand Marais. Some of the factors were: the Grand Hotel on the northeast corner of Wisconsin Street and First Avenue West had burned to the ground in October of 1908; the lot on the southeast corner of Wisconsin and First Avenue West was available; the sawmill boarding house was for sale and moveable; the need for additional hotel rooms in Grand Marais was increasing; and Mr. and Mrs. Paine had experience in the hotel business in Grand Marais.[i] With these factors evident, and probably other personal factors, Mr. Paine proceeded to purchase the sawmill boarding house on the west side of the harbor and had it moved to the site that later became the site of the Blue Water Cafe.[8]

An article in the local paper reported that:

> ...the old hotel (apparently meaning the boarding house) will be put on the back end of the lots, and a new structure will be erected in the spring...."[9] In an oral history taped in 1978 of a conversation with F. C. "Cac" Hussey, Mr. Hussey confirms the above story about the boarding house and added that the boarding house was moved by horses to its new site at First Avenue West and stated that "his parents [had] managed the boarding house [at one time]."[10] Which months Mrs. Hussey managed the boarding house is not clear. It is known that Mr. And Mrs. Dick Russell took over managing the boarding house in August of 1905.[11]

[i] The details of Mr. and Mrs. Paine's hotel experience in Grand Marais are covered in Chapter 3.

Paines Purchase Hotel Site

A view of the Hotel Paine on the southeast corner of Wisconsin and First Ave. W. The deck and balcony side is facing west toward the current Harbor Park. *Circa 1909. (Photo Courtesy of the Cook County Historical Society.)*

In June 1909, Fred Paine purchased the northern 125 feet of two lots on the southeast corner of Wisconsin and First Avenue West. Both lots were 25 feet wide and 125 feet in length. The first lot purchased was Lot 21, located 25 feet east of First Avenue West, and was purchased on June 19, 1909, from D. B. McAlpine, a Trustee of the Village of Grand Marais.[12] This is the lot on which part of Leng's Theater building stands. For some unknown reason this lot had been conveyed to the Village by the Grand Marais Real Estate and Improvement Company on February 17, 1909. The second lot, which was the northern 125 feet of the lot on the corner of Wisconsin and First Avenue West, was purchased by Fred Paine on June 23, 1909, from the Grand Marais Real Estate and Improvement Company.[13]

The timing of the documented legal purchase dates for the property was unusual, because, on February 4, 1909, the local newspaper had announced that the Paine Hotel was ready for occupancy.[14] One must assume that Fred Paine had worked out some agreements with the previous land owners that were never recorded in order for him to move the boarding house onto the site and open it as a hotel prior to signing the Warranty Deeds for the lots.

On the same day that Fred Paine signed the Warranty Deed for the first lot, he mortgaged the land to the Fitger Brewing Company for a loan of $1,000.[15] This loan apparently was to help pay for the lots and perhaps to help finance the remodeling of the boarding house into a hotel.

In the above picture the wing at the end of the building was facing Wisconsin Street. This wing must have been added after the building was moved from the east side of the harbor, because no rear wing is evident in any pictures of the sawmill boarding house. The wing may be what Mr. Paine had in mind when he was quoted in *Cook County News-Herald* dated December 24, 1908, saying: "...a new structure will be erected in the spring."[16]

It should be noted that the building in the

An early view of the Hotel Paine. The side with the stairway is facing south toward what is now the Lake Superior Trading Post. *(Photo courtesy of the Cook County Historical Society.)*

HOTEL PAINE

FRED PAINE, Prop.

New Furnishings.

Newly Painted and Papered.

First class Cafe and Buffet in connection.

Rates: $1.00, $1.50 and $2.00.

Copy of Hotel Paine advertisement first published in March 25, 1909 in the *Cook County News-Herald* The same ad ran weekly through December 1, 1910.

Copy of new ad in the *Cook County News-Herald,* dated December 15, 1910. The ad ran weekly for about five years.

A Birdseye View of Grand Marais. Note enlarged Paine Hotel in photo. *Circa 1910.* (Photo Courtesy *Cook County Historical Society.*) Identity of buildings in photo: (1) Hotel Paine, (2), Johnson's Place, (3) John Johnson's Barn, (4) John Lundin's building, (5) John Lundin's residence, (6) Lighthouse Keeper's Residence, currently Cook County Historical Society Museum, (7) Broadway Hotel, (8) Olson Bros. Livery Stable, and (9) Cook County Bank.

The Hotel Paine, Note that First Avenue West does not extend south of Wisconsin Street like it does today. Peter Alm's store is on the left in the picture. *Circa 1917. (Photo courtesy of Cook County Historical Society.)*

above photo is located somewhat south from Wisconsin Street and closer to the Lake. This left space on the north of the building to be used for the addition, which was completed in 1910.

On June 14, 1910, Fred P. Paine and his wife Mary borrowed another $2,000 from the Fitger Brewing Company using the same land as collateral.[17] This loan must have been to help the Paines enlarge the hotel. On December 15, 1910, Mr. Paine ran a new ad with a photo of the enlarged hotel in the local paper. This enlargement added space to the first and second floor of the building making it a roughly square structure and a third floor to the entire building. This was truly a significant addition to the original hotel.

The Paines Purchase Adjacent Parcels

On May 22, 1911, Mr. and Mrs. Fred Paine paid off the first mortgage for $1,000 on the hotel, which they had taken out in June 1909.[18] Approximately a year later on June 24, 1912, Fred Paine purchased the southern 125 feet of Lot 21 from D. B. McAlpine, Trustee of the Village of Grand Marais.[19] This parcel is the land on which the back half [east half] of the Lake Superior Trading Post is located.

On September 7, 1916, the Paines satisfied the second mortgage of $2,000, which they had taken out in June of 1910.[20] The satisfaction of this loan indicates that the business had been going well for the Paines. In the spring of 1918, the Paines installed a

Delco electric lighting system in the hotel.[21] This apparently was the first use of electricity in the hotel. The Grand Marais Light and Power Plant did not begin operating until February of 1921.[22]

On April 22, 1919, Fred Paine made his last purchase of land adjacent to his current lots at the corner of Wisconsin Street and First Avenue West.[23] This purchase included the northern 150 feet of lot 22, which was the third 25-foot wide lot east of First Avenue West fronting on Wisconsin Street.

The northern part of the lot is the land on which the eastern half of Leng's old theater building is located. Fred Paine purchased the parcel from Ruth Soderberg, a Grand Marais resident, who had purchased the parcel from The Cook County State Bank on June 3, 1913. The Cook County State Bank obtained all of Lot 22 from D. B. McAlpine, Trustee of the Village of Grand Marais, who had obtained it from the Grand Marais Real Estate and Improvement Company on December 28, 1910.

Mrs. Fred Paine Dies

In the fall of 1919, Mrs. Fred Paine fell from a stepladder and injured her back. She never regained her health after the fall. In late January or early February of 1920, she went to Duluth to see a doctor and it was determined that Mrs. Paine needed an operation. Unfortunately, she died in the Duluth hospital on about February 15, 1920, following the operation.[24] This left Fred Paine

Wisconsin Street Looking East. Left to right on left side of street: Trading Post, Dr. Hick's Building,[i] Bank and Johnson's New Place. Tourist Hotel on right. *Circa 1924. (Photo courtesy of Cook County Historical Society.)*

[i] Dr. F. B. Hicks, a physician, had his office on the second floor and his son, Dr. Harvey Hicks, a dentist, had his office on the first floor. In 1926 the U.S. Forest Service used part or the entire 2nd floor.

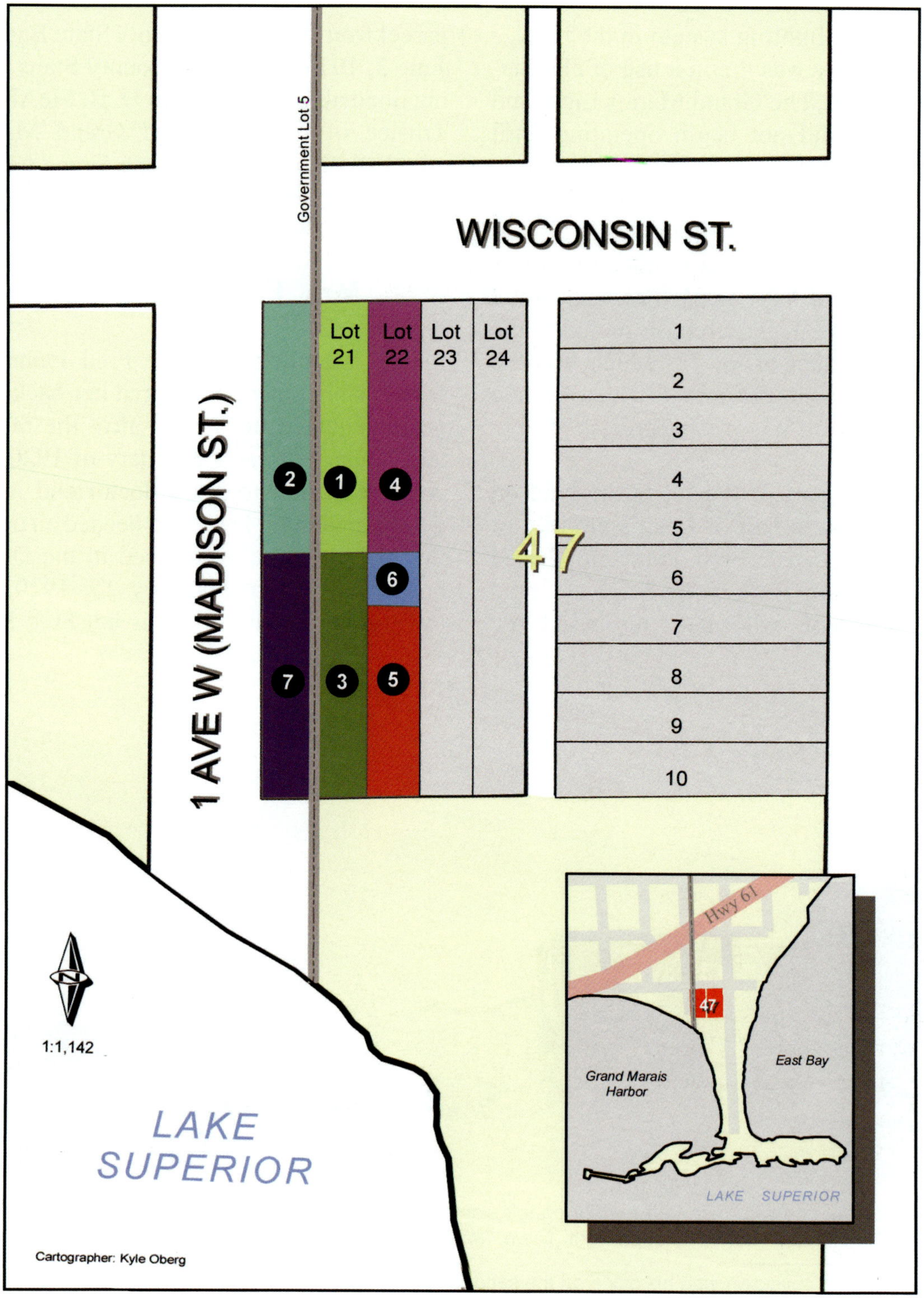

Map of southeast corner of Wisconsin and 1st Avenue west. *(Map courtesy of Kyle Oberg, Cartographer)*

< Legend of Map of Paine Hotel Area (opposite):

---

1. Fred Paine purchased the northern 125 feet of lot 21 from D. B. McAlpine, Trustee of Village of Grand Marais on June 19, 1909.

2. Corner lot, which was the easterly side of Government Lot 5 Section 21, in Township sixty-one, North range 1, east of the Fourth Principal Meridian intersected by the easterly side of Madison Street. Fred Paine purchased this 25 foot by 125 foot lot from the Grand Marais Realty Company on June 23, 1909.

3. Fred Paine purchased south 125 feet of Lot 21 from D. B. McAlpine, Trustee of Village of Grand Marais on June 24, 1912. Later it became the easterly half of the Lake Superior Trading Post.

4, 5 & 6. D. B. McAlpine, Trustee of Village of Grand Marais purchased from Grand Marais Real Estate and Improvement Company all of lot 22 on December 28, 1910. D. B. McAlpine, Trustee of the Village sold the lot to Cook County State Bank on January 12, 1911.

4 & 6. Cook County State Bank sold lot 22, except the southern 100 feet to Ruth Soderberg on June 3, 1913 for $300.00. Ruth Soderberg sold this parcel to Fred Paine on April 22, 1919.

1,2,3,4,5 & 6. Parcels Fred Paine sold to J. E. Spooner and Frederick Andert on May 25, 1920. On May 21, 1937. J. E. Spooner and Mr. and Mrs. Andert sold the same parcels to Ray and Mabel Sjoberg.

to manage the hotel by himself. Mrs. Paine had undoubtedly performed a big share of the hotel management and her death appears to have prompted Mr. Paine to sell the hotel.

Name Changes to the Tourist Hotel

On May 25, 1920, Fred Paine sold the hotel and the parcel of land he had acquired near the hotel to Mrs. J. E. Spooner and Fredrick A. Andert and Edna E. Andert.[25] Mrs. Andert was the daughter of Mrs. Spooner. Mr. and Mrs. Andert lived in Devils Lake, North Dakota prior to purchasing the Paine Hotel.[26]We know that Mrs. Spooner was living in Grand Marais at the time because she was the high school principal and a teacher from September 1917[27] and at least through May 1922.[28] The new owners changed the name of the hotel to the Tourist Hotel. By 1922, they had made several improvements

A postcard of the Paine Hotel. The car is parked on what is today First Avenue West. This picture supports the opinion that the Paine Hotel was located on the southern portion of the lot. *Circa 1919.*

in the hotel including modernizing the plumbing, providing softer beds and a recreation room.[29] In the fall of 1922, Mr. Andert accepted the position of Superintendent of the local school in Grand Marais. He held this position until he resigned effective September 1, 1946. The career change for Fredrick Andert obviously meant that the primary management of the Tourist Hotel was left to Mrs. Spooner and Mrs. Andert.

The New Grand Marais Hotel

In August of 1922, the local newspaper reported that during the summers of 1921 and 1922 the local hotel accommodations were taxed to the limit and it was anticipated that the number of visitors to Grand Marais would increase in the years to come. In this same article the newspaper editorialized as follows:

> This influx of high class travel [sic traveler] far exceeds the effort being made to handle it. These people want comfort at the end of the day's journey. They want water and plenty of it: they want a bath and a good dinner. Furthermore they are willing to pay for it. There is no class of travel [sic traveler] more worth catering to than the summer tourist. He has money and expects to spend it. The better the accommodations offered, the more cheerfully he will pay for it.[30]

For these reasons the local papers claimed that Mrs. Spooner and the Anderts had begun building one of the finest tourist hotels in the North Country.

This new Grand Marais Hotel was to have eighty good sized rooms.

Tourist Hotel. *Circa 1929. (Photo Courtesy of Cook County Historical Museum.)*

> Every room will have hot and cold water. Fifteen shower baths are provided and a sufficient number of tubs. Several rooms are furnished with private bathrooms. Every room is an outside room fronting either on the harbor or looking into the pine woods. A large lobby, comfortably furnished, a spacious dining room and a commodious kitchen make up the balance of the hotel.[31]

This same August 21, 1922, article announced that the foundation of the building was completed and work was to begin on the main structure that week and was to cost $65,000.

The article does not explain where the hotel was located, but we now know that the site of the proposed hotel was the land behind the current Java Moose Coffee Shop east to Second Avenue West and between Wisconsin Street and Highway 61. This is the parcel where the Harbor Inn Motel and Omega Land & Abstract Company office is currently located.

In November 1921, Mrs. J. E. Spooner and Mr. Frederick Andert had purchased this land, plus the land on which the Java Moose is located, from the Grand Marais Realty Company.[32] It should also be noted that these lots extended further north than they do today, because highway 61 did not exist in its present location until the 1930's. On July 15, 1922, Mrs. Spooner and Mr. Andert entered into a mortgage agreement with the Grand Marais State Bank for up to $60,000, based on the sale of bonds for their new hotel.[33] The local newspaper indicated that Messrs. Randall & Dunn, of Duluth were issuing bonds.[34] Additional evidence that the building of the hotel had begun was the outline and notation of a foundation for a large building on a Highway 61 survey map dated about 1930, and comments by several people who remember the foundation being there in the thirties and forties.

There is no evidence that anything was ever built on the foundation. What caused a halt in the construction of the hotel is not known today. Perhaps the bonds did not sell or perhaps it was because Frederick Andert accepted the position of school superintendent in the fall of 1922, and decided not to go forward with the new hotel venture. Or, maybe Mr. Andert accepted the school position because the hotel venture fell through. At this point in time we can only speculate about what may have caused Mrs. Spooner and Mr. Andert to halt construction on their new hotel.

Now Open for Business

When Your friends come to Grand Marais be sure to have them stop at

The Tourist Hotel

Where Home Comforts Await Them

WE AIM TO PLEASE

Hot & Cold Running Water
in Every Room, Baths. Meals that are Home Cooked.

GUIDES WANTED
Persons wishing to act as guides for fishing or canoeing parties kindly file your name with the TOURIST HOTEL

Advertisement in *Cook County News-Herald*, April 23, 1925. p. 4.

Regardless of what caused the halt in the construction of the Grand Marais Hotel, the Anderts and Mrs. Spooner shifted gears and remodeled their Tourist Hotel in the fall of 1924 and early 1925. Sometime during this period the hotel was closed for remodeling and re-opened in April 1925. At the time they ran a large advertisement announcing the re-opening of the hotel.

Tourist Hotel Destroyed by Fire

The end of the Tourist Hotel came on December 31, 1931, when fire destroyed the building. This was the fourth hotel to be destroyed by fire in Grand Marais between 1908 and 1931. Fires also destroyed numerous other buildings in Grand

Tourist Hotel Fire, December 31, 1931

Marais during this period. All the buildings were of wood frame or log construction. Some of the causes of the early fires were the use of oil lamps for light, wood stoves, and in later years improper electrical wiring. The primitive fire fighting equipment of this period also made it very difficult to contain a fire once it was started.

The lots where the Tourist Hotel was located remained vacant for a number of years. Following the fire, Mrs. Spooner and the Anderts went into the cabin business and built the Birches, on Fifth Avenue West and First Street. These cabins are now called Russell's Cabins. Mr. Andert continued as Superintendent of the local school and also taught a math class. Mr. and Mrs. Andert lived in the house on the northwest corner of the property, and Mrs. Spooner lived in a log cabin in the summer and moved into the house in the winter. [34]

During the summer of 1946, Mr. Andert resigned his school position.[35] In October, Mr. and Mrs. Andert, and Mrs. J. E. Spooner left Grand Marais for Santa Monica, California, a suburb of Los Angeles, where Mr. Andert had accepted a position as a mathematics and science teacher.[36] In 1948 Mr. and Mrs. Robert Russell purchased the Birches and changed the name to Russell's Cabins. Whether the cabins were open during the summers of 1947 and 1948 is not clear. The Anderts may have hired someone to manage the cabins for them during these summers. Currently Joyce Russell Lindquist, a daughter of Mr. and Mrs. Russell owns and manages the Russell Cabins, with her husband Gordon.

(Endnotes)

1. "New Mill for Grand Marais," *Cook County Herald*, December 5, 1903, p. 3.

2. *Cook County Herald*, June 17, 1905, p. 5.

3. *Cook County Herald*, July 22, 1905, p. 6.

4. Willis H. Raff, *Pioneers in the Wilderness* (Grand Marais, MN: Cook County Historical Society, 1981), pp. 362-367.

5. Book I, Deed Record, p. 116, Recorders Office, Cook County Court House, Grand Marais, MN.

6. Book G, Quit Claim Deed Record, p. 340, Recorders Office, Cook County Court House, Grand Marais, MN.

7. Book Z, Quit Claim Deed Record, p. 151, Recorders Office, Cook County Court House, Grand Marais, MN.

8. *Cook County News-Herald*, December 24, 1908.

9. *Cook County News-Herald*, December 24, 1908.

10. "Overlook", *Cook County Historical Society*, June 2000, p. 5.

11. "Topics of a Week," *Cook County Herald*, August 12, 1905, p. 5.

12. Book R, Deed Record, p. 24, Recorders Office, Cook County Court House, Grand Marais, MN.

13. Book Q, Deed Record, p. 24, Recorders Office, Cook County Court House, Grand Marais, MN.

14. "Topics of a Week," *Cook County Herald*, February 18, 1909.

15. Book D, Mortgages p.150, Recorders Office, Cook County Court House, Grand Marais, MN.

16. *Cook County News Herald,* December 24, 1908.

17. Book D, Mortgages p.267, Recorders Office, Cook County Court House, Grand Marais, MN.

18. Book F, Mortgages p.466, Recorders Office, Cook County Court House, Grand Marais, MN.

19. Book R, Deed Record, P. 274, Recorders Office, Cook County Court House, Grand Marais, MN.

20. Book D, Mortgage Record p.368, Recorders Office, Cook County Court House, Grand Marais, MN.

21. *Cook County News-Herald*, May 8, 1918.

22. "THE GRAND MARAIS LIGHT AND POWER PLANT," *Cook County News-Herald*, February 3, 1921. p.1.

23. Book 1, Warranty Deed Record, p.385, Recorders Office, Cook County Court House, Grand Marais, MN.

24. "MRS. F. R. PAINE DIED MONDAY At DULUTH," *Cook County News-Herald*, February 18, 1920. p.1.

25. Book 1, Deed Record, p. 524, Recorders Office, Cook County Court House, Grand Marais, MN.

26. "News-ettes of Grand Marais and Vicinity," *Cook County News-Herald*, May 19, 1920. p.1.

27. "LOCAL SCHOOLS OPENED WITH LARGE ENROLLMENT," *Cook County News-Herald*, September 5, 1917. p.1.

28. "SCHOOL NOTES," *Cook County News-Herald*, November 29, 1921, p.1.

29. "WORK TO START ON NEW HOTEL," *Cook County News-Herald*, August 24, 1922, p.1.

30. "WORK TO START ON NEW HOTEL," *Cook County News-Herald*, August 24, 1922, p.1.

31. Ibid

32. Book 5, Warrant Deed Record, p. 38, Recorders Office, Cook County Court House, Grand Marais, MN.

33. Book 2, Mortgage Record, p. 263-267, Recorders Office, Cook County Court House, Grand Marais, MN.

34. Interview with Joyce Russell Lindquist, July 6, 2007.

35. "F. A. ANDERT RESIGNS POST," *Cook County News-Herald*, July 25, 1946, p. 1.

36. "The Anderts in Transit For California," *Cook County News-Herald*, October 10, 1946, p. 1.

Chapter 3

Corner Business Changes from Hotel to Cafe

Tony's Eat

On May 21, 1937, Mr. and Mrs. Andert and Mrs. Spooner sold the land on which the Tourist Hotel had been located, and other adjacent land, they owned, to Ray and Mabel Sjoberg.[1] About two weeks later, Mr. and Mrs. Sjoberg sold the north 125 feet of Lots 21 and 22 to Loren and Irene Leng.[2] It was on this land that the Lengs built the Shore Theater. This sale included a 10-foot easement across the back of what became known as the Blue Water Cafe lot, so that the Lengs

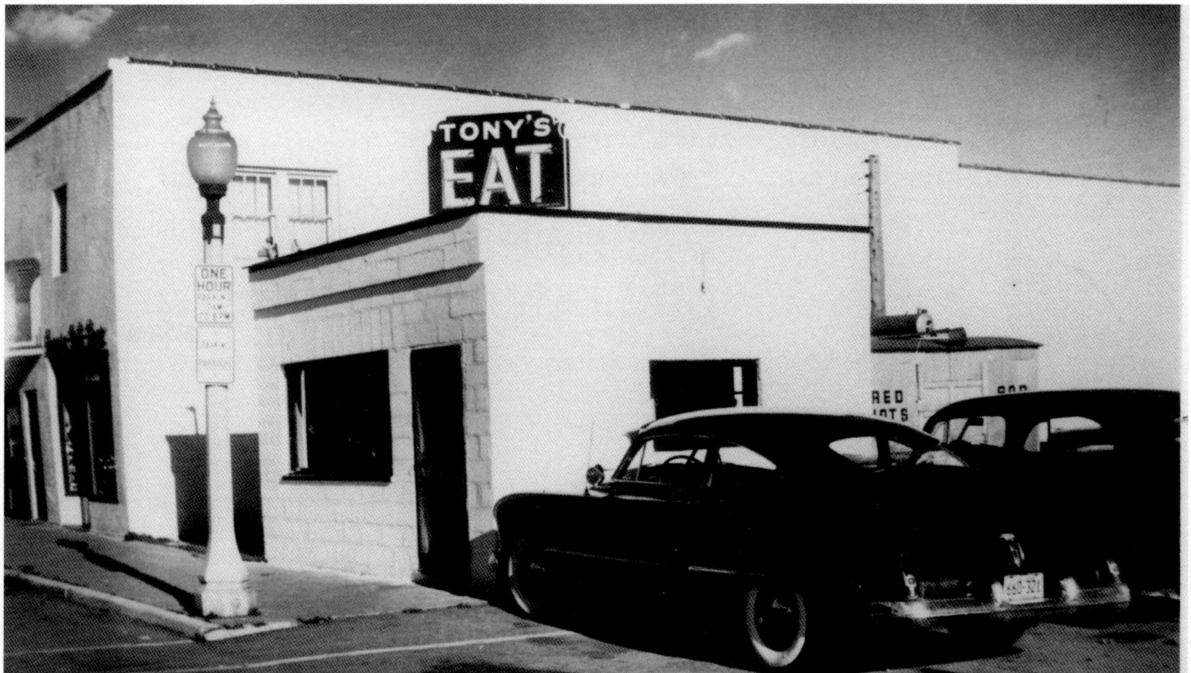

Tony's Eat. C*irca 1948, (Photo courtesy of Cook County Historical Museum.)*

would have access to the south end of their lot.

About 1946, Vic Cartier rented the corner-lot from the Sjobergs and built a small cafe called "Tony's Eat" on the parcel. It was a small operation with five or six stools at a counter.

By December 1948, the name of the cafe had been changed to "Tony's Lunch," according to an advertisement in the local paper.[3] In 1951 or early 1952, the building was moved to the lot on the east side of the Shore Theater.[4] That was the lot where the Sjoberg Restaurant was located until it burned down in December 1934.[5] Fred Sjoberg, who was a brother to Ray Sjoberg Sr. had owned and operated the Sjoberg Restaurant. In 1954, the name of Tony's Lunch was changed to Chris's Eat Shop. The end of the eat shop came sometime before 1957 when Milford and Ed Humphrey built a new clothing store on the site.[6] The building currently houses the Sivertson Gallery.

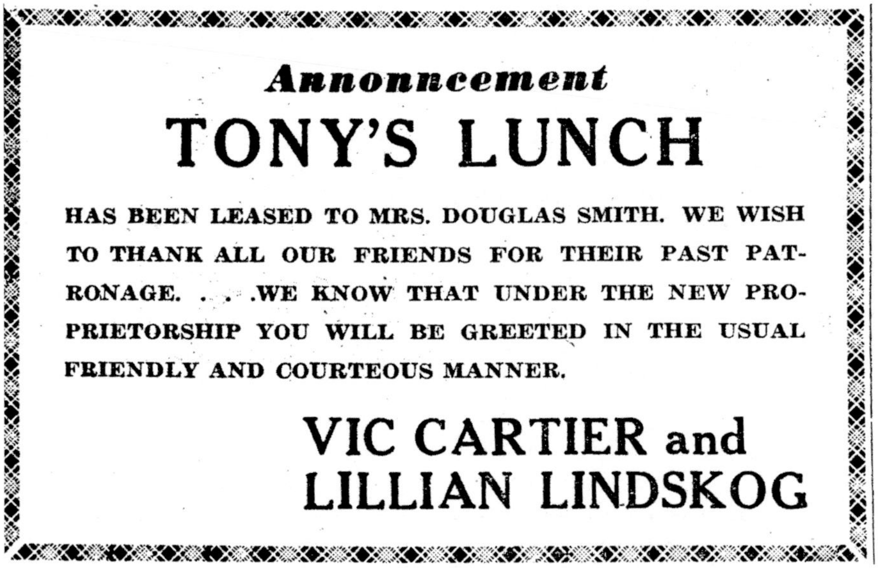

Advertisement in *Cook County News-Herald* on September 11, 1952.

Wisconsin Street. Right to Left: Du Nord Cafe, Shore Theater, Tony's Lunch after it was moved, A building housing Henry Rindahl Watch Repair Business in the front corner and Toftey Propane Gas in rear, The sign on the front of the building reads "Your Grocer Ed Toftey." and some words too small to decifer. The next buildings are the Toftey IGA Supermarket and the Pioneer House. *Circa 1954. (Photo Courtesy of Charles Humphrey.)*

Chris's Eat Shop

(formerly Tony's Lunch)

IS OPEN FROM 11 A. M. TO 1 A. M.

24 HOUR SERVICE DURING DEER SEASON

Advertisement in *Cook County News-Herald*
September 12, 1954, p. 8.

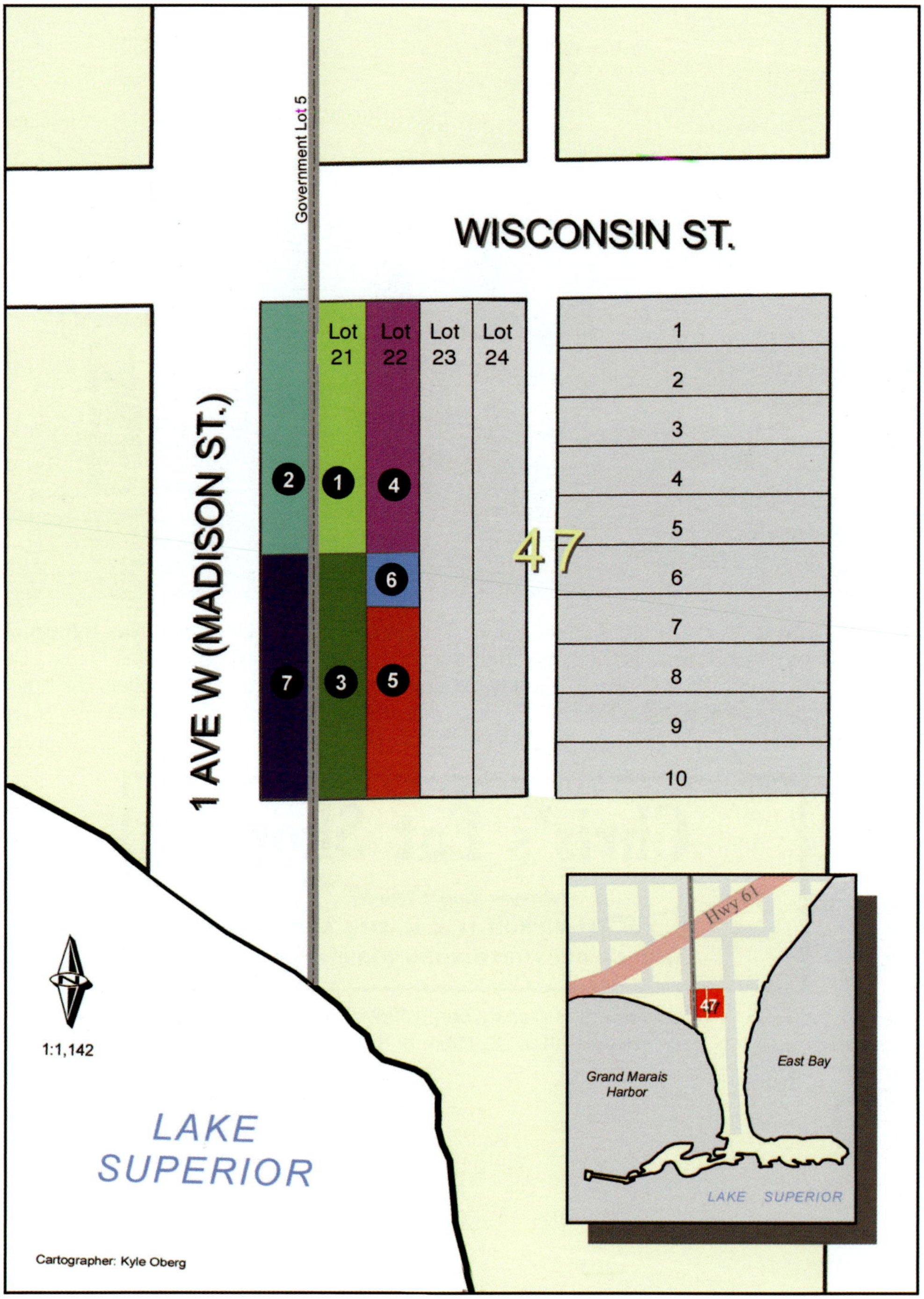

Map of the Blue Water Cafe and Lake Superior Trading PostArea. *(Map courtesy of Kyle Oberg, Cartographer.)*

Legend for Blue Water Cafe, Trading Post and Theater Map (Opposite Page)

#1 & 4 Ray & Mabel Sjoberg sold the northern 125 feet of lots 21 & 22 to Loren & Irene Leng on July 3, 1937.

7 Ray Sjoberg purchased this parcel from E. E. and Marguerite Johnson on March 21, 1938.

3 & 7 Sidney Kluck and Cyril Kluck purchased these parcels from Ray Sjoberg on August 8, 1940.

3 & 7 Edward and Lillian Anderson purchased these parcels from Cyril Kluck on July 4, 1964.

3 & 7 Edward A. and John U. Viren purchased these parcels from Edward and Lillian Anderson on January 18, 1971.

2 Ray Sjoberg built the cafe on this lot in 1952. Note: A 25 x 25 foot parcel, # 6 in the diagram, remained part of the cafe property. Currently the Blue Water Cafe's propane tanks are located on this parcel.

The Du Nord Opens

In March of 1952, Ray Sjoberg Sr. and Ray Sjoberg Jr. began building a new cafe on the corner of Wisconsin Street and First Avenue West, where "Tony's Eats" had stood.[7] The building included an apartment on the second floor where Mr. and Mrs. Ray Sjoberg Sr. lived until about the mid 1960's. In the late sixties and/or early seventies the second floor was rented out as office space.

The Sjobergs operated the new cafe for a short time in 1952 and then leased it in the late summer or fall of 1952 to Frank and Thelma (Sally) Rosener. The Roseners

Postcard photo of Cafe Du Nord. *Circa 1953.*

Postcard photo of Cafe Du Nord. *Circa 1953.*

called the cafe the Du Nord, which had been the name of a cafe they had in Minneapolis.[8] The Roseners had previously leased Jackson's Cafe in Grand Marais in 1946,[9]

Hamburger and
French Fries In a Basket 50c
Du Nord

Advertisement in the *Cook County News-Herald*, September 10, 1953, p. 6.

Fried Chicken
in a basket $1.25

Advertisement in the *Cook County News-Herald*, September 17, 1953, p. 6.

and had opened a cafe called Spruce Harbor in Lutsen in July of 1947.[10]

In October 1953, about a year after leasing the cafe, Frank Rosener suddenly died while working behind the counter in the cafe.[11] Mrs. Thelma (Sally) Rosener continued to operate the Du Nord after her husband's

Bar-be-cued Ribs, French Fries
Salad and Beverage . . . $1.25
Du Nord

Advertisement in the *Cook County News-Herald*, September 24, 1953, p. 6

death, until November 1956. During the month prior to Mr. Roseners' death they ran the advertisements on the previous page in the *Cook County News-Herald* which illustrate the menu and prices in 1953.

Advertisement in the *Cook County News-Herald*, April 15, 1954, p.2.

In March of 1954, Mrs. Rosener undertook some remodeling of the cafe, but kept it open. The remodeling included an addition to the back of the building and moving the kitchen and baking facilities to the new space. With the space vacated by moving the kitchen, a room called the "Trapper Room" was created. This room could accommodate fourteen people for meetings and private parties.[12] Another part of the remodeling included the painting of a map of Lake Superior on the east wall by high school art students.

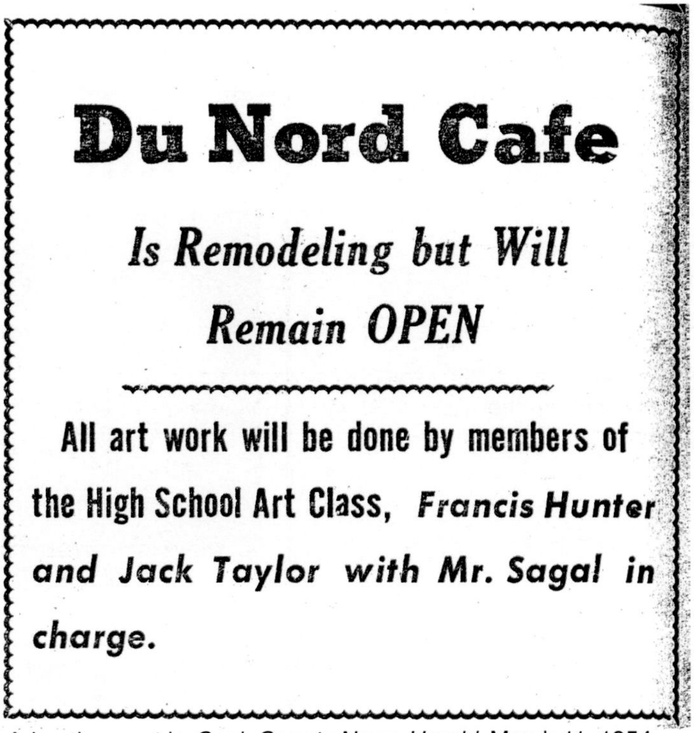

Advertisement in *Cook County News-Herald*, March 11, 1954, p. 6.

About 1953, when a few pizza restaurants were emerging in Minnesota Mrs. Rosener capitalized on this new menu item and began selling "Italian Pizza Pie" in November of 1955. This was the first advertising for pizza by any restaurant in the *Cook County News-Herald*. Free delivery in the village of Grand Marais was included in the very first "Pizza Pie" advertisement. In February, the ads included a picture of an Italian Pizza Pie.

In November 1956, Amy Hussey took over the cafe for a short time and renamed it Amy's Cafe. At this time the Husseys also owned and managed Naniboujou Lodge, which they had purchased in 1953.[13] The lodge was most likely closed during the winter, which allowed them to operate the cafe in Grand Marais at this time

The first advertisement for pizza by the Du Nord Cafe in the *Cook County News-Herald* was on November 10, 1955.

Advertisement in *Cook County News-Herald*, February 16, 1956, p. 4

Cafe Renamed the El Ray Cafe

In March of 1957, Ray Sjoberg Jr., and his wife Eleanor, became proprietors of the cafe and renamed it the El Ray Cafe. They closed the cafe for a week in April for some remodeling and reopened on April 25, 1957. The remodeling included installing a new ceiling, new light fixtures, booths, tables and repainting the map of Lake Superior on the wall.[14] In 1968, a Warranty Deed from his parents officially gave Ray W. and Eleanor Sjoberg title to the cafe.

Advertisement in the *Cook County News-Herald*, November 1, 1956, p. 10.

The El Ray Cafe. *Circa 1960. (Photo courtesy of Kenny Lovaas.)*

The El Ray Cafe is Sold

On November 30, 1973, the Sjobergs sold the cafe to Blue Water, Inc. The principal owners of Blue Water, Inc., were Michael and Sharon Rusten, who were the principal owners of Cascade Lodge. Sharon Rusten is the daughter of Carl and Mae Odmark, who were also involved in the cafe operation. The cafe was renamed the Blue Water Cafe at this time. During the late fall and early winter of 1974-75 the dining area of the cafe was remodeled and redecorated. The remodeling included installing a new counter, wallpapering the walls, new curtains, placing many pictures of earlier days on the walls, creating a new logo and new signage. The new wallpaper covered the painted map of Lake Superior on the east wall. The remodeling included adding a twenty-five foot addition to the back of the building for increased kitchen and storage space, and an office.

Photo of Ray and Eleanor Sjoberg and Donald Dewey, the new manager of the renamed Blue Water Cafe. (Photo by M. J. Humphrey in *Cook County News-Herald*, December 6, 1973.)

Bill Thomas, who was managing the Cascade Lodge Restaurant was given responsibility for establishing the menu and overall supervision of the food and service at the cafe. Don Dewey was hired as the new on-site manager. Don had graduated from the University of Minnesota where he had majored in hospitality and food service management and was currently working at the Curtis Hotel in Minneapolis. [15]

Original Lake Superior map in the Blue Water Cafe. *Circa 1958. Postcard courtesy of Bill and Beth Blank.*

Blue Water Cafe

The New Logo

Communion at the Blue Water

Birney Quick, a local artist and the founder of the Grand Marais Art Colony was a frequent participant in coffee shop discussions at the Blue Water Cafe during the seventies. Based on his experiences at the cafe he painted a wonderful picture entitled "Communion at the Blue Water Cafe" in 1976. The painting currently hangs in the Congregational Church in Grand Marais.

A photo of "Communion at the Blue Water Cafe" by Birney Quick.

A photo of the painting was part of a very nice tribute to Birney Quick in the *Cook County News-Herald* on December 10, 1981. The following quote is a paragraph from this article.

"'Communion at the Blue Water Cafe,' painted by Birney Quick in 1976, was donated to the First Congregational Church on Sunday, November 27, by Robert and Mary Jane Bowen. They had bought the painting from Birney and had wanted to see it hung in the church. The painting, they felt, as did Birney, represents a Christ figure doing what everyone does. He is depicted as an approachable figure; you can sit next to Christ as you can with anyone. The use of Christian symbols is also evident in the painting; the breaking of bread, fish and money."[16]

The picture is full of symbolism and is worth contemplating as one fellowships with friends over a cup of coffee or around a table laden with food. As previous owners of the Cafe, providing a place for people to experience fellowship was one of the satisfactions of being in the hospitality business.

The Cafe is Sold Again

On July 29, 1981, the cafe was sold to Cascade Lodge Associates and Cascade Lodge, Inc.

A group of locals and seasonal residents who gathered for coffee and fellowship daily during the summer of 2007 posing for a photo: Seated left to right: Roy Mark, Jerry Peterson, Duncan McDonald, Standing left to right: Gene Pearson, Chuck Tice, Alton Berglund and Allen Clothier. *(Photo by Jim Ringquist.)*

the new owners of Cascade Lodge. Gene and Laurene Glader were the principal officers of both business entities. By 1981 Don Dewey had left the area and Bill Thomas was managing both the Blue Water Cafe and the Cascade Lodge Restaurant. Bill continued on in this capacity until he and his wife, Lois, retired in 1986.

In the early days of our ownership we were very impressed with the number of locals and tourists who came to the Blue Water Cafe for coffee and meals and how frequently we heard people say, "I'll meet you at the Blue Water." These observations prompted us to adopt the phrase "The Meeting Place in Grand Marais!" as the cafe slogan.

Coffee Cup with slogan "The Meeting Place in Grand Marais."

Blue Water Cafe. Note the 1974 addition to the kitchen area in the rear of the restaurant. *Circa 1981.*

After the change in ownership in 1973, the second floor was used for storage and occasionally rented out for gift shop space in the summer. After purchasing the cafe in 1981, we rented the second floor to a gift shop proprietor during the summer of 1982. At this time customers used the side door and stairway to get to the second floor. We also tried selling some gift shop items ourselves in a room on the second floor as an extension of the Cascade Lodge Gift Shop. The success of the gift shop ventures were modest at best.

Gift Shop advertisement in *Cook County News-Herald* in July, August and September 1982.

By 1983, the decision was made to remodel the second floor of the cafe into a restaurant area. Larry Krause, a local contractor, was hired to do the remodeling. The remodeling involved replacing all the second floor windows and removing two interior walls, adding rough wood paneling to some interior walls and converting one room to a small new kitchen/waitress station area. The new upstairs was called the Upper Deck.

The Blue Water Cafe. Note Upper Deck entrance on the right. *Fall 1983.*

With the new windows, the view of the town, harbor and hills was spectacular. Jim Ringquist, owner of Times Two Design in Grand Marais, designed an Upper Deck logo for us and constructed the sign and facade at the entrance.

Originally the Upper Deck menu had an emphasis on Italian dishes. Some of the food was prepared in the new, but small upstairs kitchen and some in the Blue Water kitchen on the first floor.

Guests had to come in the side door and climb a flight of stairs to the Upper Deck. All the service personnel had to use the same stairway for carrying food and dishes to and from the down stairs kitchen. For orders filled in the down stairs kitchen a wait staff person had to run the order slip down to the kitchen, go back up and wait on other tables and then go back down stairs again when the order was ready. On busy days the

Advertisement in *Cook County News-Herald* on June 2, 1983.

New restaurant opens in Grand Marais

Interior photo of Upper Deck when it opened on May 24, 1983. (The photo is a copy of a picture in the *Cook County News-Herald* on June 2, 1983. p. 11.)

UPPER DECK FORUM

Wednesdays Oct. 9 - Nov. 27, 12:05 - 12:55 p.m.

This new program will enable you to learn more about issues of importance to our County. Each Wednesday, the chosen speaker will comment on a topic for 20 minutes followed by a 20 minute discussion and wrap up. Soup, sandwich, and beverage available, or bring a bag lunch and spend your Wednesday noon hours at the Upper Deck. The first four topics are:

Oct. 9:	Bruce Kerfoot; School Board Member report on the Long-range Planning Committee for Cook County Schools
Oct. 16:	Warren Rolek; Superintendent of Schools School Referendum
Oct. 23:	Walt Mianowski: Mayor of Grand Marais Planned use of the Transferred Consolidated Paper Co. Land by the City of Grand Marais.
Oct. 30:	Edward McMillan: Acting Hospital Administrator The Future of the Hospital in Cook County

All programs will begin and end on time.
Sponsored by Community Ed. and the Upper Deck.

The first advertisement for the Upper Deck Forum in the *Cook County News-Herald*, October 3, 1985.

traffic on the stairway was crazy. In spite of some problems in creating the new dining area, the added dining space, with a view, proved to be an asset that should be further developed. Because there was a shortage of private restaurant rooms in Grand Marais at the time, many small groups found the Upper Deck a good place for meetings.

The Upper Deck Forum

In the fall of 1985, the Upper Deck Forum was established. The idea for the forum came to me while listening to a presentation/discussion program on a Twin Cities Public Radio Station. I thought the type of program I had heard would be a good concept and format to try in Grand Marais. A few days later I discussed the concept with Burt Kreitlow, a retired professor from the University of Wisconsin, and he thought it had potential and suggested that we present the idea to Jane Brumberg, who at the time was Director of Community Education at the school. Jane's response was positive and with her support and cooperation we started a series of presentations and discussions that became known as the Upper Deck Forum. Burt moderated many of the sessions during the first years. Some of the other people who served as moderators were Robert Hattery, Paul Anderson, Robert Pye, and Bill Hanson.

The meetings were held during the school year and started at 12:05 p.m. and lasted for 50 minutes. The format for the meetings was as follows: The Upper Deck Restaurant provided a simple lunch option of soup, sandwich, dessert and beverage, or one could bring a bag lunch. At 12:05 a moderator would introduce a speaker or speakers, who would make a presentation for 20-25 minutes. Then there was 20 minutes for discussion, followed by five minutes of concluding comments by the speaker and/or moderator. The programs would end promptly at 12:55.

In 1988, the Upper Deck Forum was awarded the Minnesota Outstanding Project Award by the State Community Education Association. This award recognized the forum as the top community education program in the state for the previous year for school districts with 20,000 or less people.[17] Jane Brumberg deserved a lot of credit for this recognition. The local newspaper announced the recognition with the headline, "Upper Deck Forum Wins State Award," an article and the photo[18] shown in the next column.

Shortly after founding the Forum, an advisory committee was formed, which helped select topics and presenters. Over the years the Forums covered a wide range of local, state and national issues. During the first four years of the Forum over 50 sessions had been held with a total of over 2,000 people in attendance. The forums were also broadcast on local cable television channel 13 through the efforts of Holly Nelson, who faithfully videotaped the programs.

Gene Glader and Jane Brumberg display the 1988 Minnesota Outstanding Project Award that was presented to the Upper Deck Forum program at the Annual Community Education Association Conference. *(Photo from Cook County News-Herald, October 31, 1988, p.1.)*

The Forum continued on a weekly basis until about the year 2000, when the program became less frequent. The Upper Deck proved to be a very good setting for the forums and the format proved to be a very interesting and helpful communication medium for the community. Robert Hattery,[1] a national authority on adult public discussion programs, stated that "the Upper Deck Forum has been a highly important and esteemed institution in the civic life of Grand Marais and Cook County, with significant spill over along the North Shore."[19]

[1] Robert Hattery, Ph.D. A retired professor emeritus of political science at Indiana University currently living in Cook County who has taught at the Universities of Indiana and Wisconsin

Interior of first floor of Blue Water Cafe after remodeling 1990. Marion Killmer and Kenny Lovaas are having coffee at the counter on July 11, 2007 in the photo.

Interior of second floor after remodeling in 1990.

Map of Lake Superior on 1st floor wall. The map was painted by Timothy Young. *2007*

Remodeling of the Cafe and Upper Deck

The next stage in the development of the Blue Water Cafe took place in the late fall of 1990. To accomplish the remodeling the cafe was closed for several weeks. At this time several changes were made in the interior layout of the first and second floors of the cafe. On the first floor the remodeling included creating a new entrance and building a new stairway to the second floor, and the installation of a new counter and lights. On the second floor a new bathroom was added, removing another interior wall and moving the furnace from the first floor to the second.

The relocating of the furnace to the second floor allowed space for moving the first floor bathrooms back toward the kitchen and thus creating more space for booths and a redesigned counter. The end result was the addition of about fifty additional seats for customers and a space on the second floor that could be used for groups and meetings as well as normal restaurant service.

Prior to this remodeling project we had been told that there used to be a map of Lake Superior painted on some wall, but we had

The Blue Water Cafe C*irca 2007*

The View from the Upper Deck after Harbor Park was finished. Photo taken July 2007.

never seen a picture of it. While doing the remodeling we discovered remnants of the old map and decided to add the map again to the decor. Tim Young, a local artist, was hired for the task. In order to get the details of the map accurate he used an overhead projector to project the outline of the lake unto the wall and he then painted in the details. The map has been a very popular addition to the decor. It is not unusual to see guests looking at the map and discussing details about the lake or their vacation.

As part of the changes made during the remodeling in 1990, a system was installed that allowed the wait staff to punch in the orders upstairs and downstairs on computers. The orders then would be printed out in the kitchen for the cooks. When the order was ready the cooks would notify the wait staff with a light system or buzzer. This system saved many steps up and down the back stairs for the wait staff. It also made the calculation of sales tax automatic on guest checks. Some additional benefits of this new system were as follows: (1) It was easier for cooks to read the printed orders, in contrast to hand written orders from the wait staff, (2) It forced the wait staff to include such things as how meat was to be done with their orders, and (3) It provided an accurate and easier to read guest check for customers.

The Riddles Purchase the Cafe

Over the years, Laurene and I bought out the other investors in the cafe. Then in 2003, we decided it was time to retire and pursue some other dreams and projects. Therefore, on May 3, 2004, we sold Cascade Lodge to Michael and Maureen O'Phelan and a year later, on May 4, 2005, sold the Blue Water Cafe to Daniel and Melodee Riddle. Dan Riddle had been hired to manage the cafe in mid December 1986, and Melodee had worked in the cafe since about 1987. It was an easy decision to sell to the Riddles. The next phase of the Blue Water Cafe history will be up to them. We wish them well. Grand Marais is a great community. We will always be thankful for the wonderful people

Dan and Melodee Riddle and Laurene and Gene Glader on May 4, 2005, the day of the sale.

Some of the employees who have worked at the Blue Water Cafe between 17 and 22 years as of 2007. Seated left to right: Melodee Riddle, Jerry Bly and Kelly Roberts. Standing left to right: Dan Riddle and William (Bill) Wissman. *2007, (Photo by Jim Ringquist.)*

who worked for us and for the multitude of customers who allowed us to serve them. We hope the Blue Water Cafe will always be "The Meeting Place in Grand Marais."

(Endnotes)

1. Book 10, Deed Record, p. 256, Recorders Office, Cook County Court House, Grand Marais, Minnesota.

2 . Book 10, Deed Record. p. 257, Recorders Office, Cook County Court House, Grand Marais, Minnesota.

3 . "Tony's Lunch Advertisement," *Cook County News-Herald*, December 23, 1948, p. 11.

4. Interview with Douglas Smith, June 6, 2007, Douglas Smith's wife leased the cafe in September 1952.

5. "Sjoberg's Restaurant Destroyed By Fire," *Cook County News-Herald*, December 27, 1934, p. 1.

6. "Humphreys Have Open House Friday," *Cook County News-Herald*, August 15, 1957, p. 1.

7. "Sjobergs Erecting Building Here," *Cook County News-Herald*, March 27, 1952, p. 1.

8. "Frank Rosener, 60 Dies Suddenly," *Cook County News-Herald*, October 22, 1953, p. 1.

9. "Jacksons Lease Restaurant," *Cook County News-Herald*, February 7, 1946, p. 1.

10. "Spruce Harbor Advertisement," *Cook County News-Herald*, July 24, 1947, p. 7.

11. "Frank Rosener, 60 Dies Suddenly," *Cook County News-Herald*, October 22, 1953, p. 1.

12. "'Trapper Room' Will Be Feature at the Du Nord," *Cook County News-Herald*, February 25, 1954, p. 1.

13. "Husseys Buy Naniboujou; To Operate Year Around," *Cook County News-Herald*, February 19, 1953, p. 1.

14. "Cafes 'Spruce Up' for Busy Summer Patronage," *Cook County News-Herald*, April 23, 1957, p. 1.

15. "El Ray Cafe Will Change Ownership On Sat.," *Cook County News-Herald*, November 29, 1973, p. 1.

16. "Tribute To Birney Quick," *Cook County News-Herald*, December 10, 1981, p. 2.

17. Upper Deck Forum Wins State Award," *Cook County News-Herald*, October 31, 1988, p. 1.

18. "Upper Deck Forum Wins State Award," Cook County News-Herald, October 31, 1988, p. 1.

19. Email from Robert "Bob" Hattery to Gene Glader, January 21, 2008.

Chapter 4

The Mayhew, Broadway and Sterling Hotels

Introduction

The research into the history of the Blue Water Cafe site led to the discovery of the Hotel Paine and Mr. and Mrs. Fred Paine's work experience in other hotels. This research led to the discovery that a Mrs. Paine, who was most likely Mrs. Fred Paine, had managed the Mayhew Hotel for a while, and the realization that Mr. and Mrs. Fred Paine had leased the Broadway Hotel for two years prior to opening their own hotel. Consequently, my interest in these two hotels was perked and thus began the process of broadening the scope of this book.

The Mayhew and Broadway Hotels not only provided hotel experience for Mr. and Mrs. Paine, the work must have also convinced them of the need for more lodging facilities in the growing Village of Grand Marais. The Paine Hotel filled the need for an additional lodging facility due to the increase in travelers to the town and the loss of the Grand Hotel by fire in 1908.

The Mayhew Hotel

The first lodging place in Grand Marais was the Mayhew Hotel on the point. In an article by Dr. F. R. Hicks, published on October 6, 1929, he quoted A. J. Scott who came to Grand Marais in 1872 as follows: "He say [sic "said"] that at that time there were only two dwelling houses in the place and one of them was the big building owned and used by Mr. Mayhew and his brother, Thomas, who had lately joined him, as [sic] the trading post, hotel and post office [sic]."[1] In 1979, Steven J. Wright, who was a historian-archivist for the Cook County Historical Society, wrote, "By 1887 Grand Marais had grown and was beginning to prosper, and the prosperity had reached to Thomas and Henry Mayhew. The brothers had built a hotel, store, and dock and warehouse along the water front."[2] The hotel was built about 1880, but it seems reasonable to assume that the Mayhew brothers were taking in boarders in their home prior to building the hotel. For a few years the front room of the hotel was the location of the first school in the county. When the hotel burned down in 1916, the building was vacant except for a

"The Point" with Mayhew's Hotel slightly right of the center of the picture. The dark, larger building left of the center is Mayhew's home, store and the Post Office. *Circa 1894.(Photo Courtesy of Cook County Historical Museum.)*

cigar factory, which was operated by George Brisson on the second floor.[3]

According to the local newspaper a Mrs. Paine was managing the Mayhew Hotel in 1899.[4] The Mrs. Paine mentioned in the article is most likely the wife of Fred R. Paine, who later owned and operated the Hotel Paine, but she may have been a relative.

The Mayhew Hotel had various unofficial names over the years, which makes getting its history correct more difficult. Sometimes the Mayhew Hotel was called the Grand Marais Hotel,[5] sometimes Mayhew's Lakeview Hotel,[6] and sometimes the Bay View, and sometimes the Waldorf.[7]

The use of the name Waldorf in the local paper was obviously used in jest. The Mayhew Hotel was a far cry from the Waldorf Hotel in New York. It must be remembered that there was no public water or sewer system and no electric lights in Grand Marais at this time, and consequently no indoor plumbing in hotel rooms.

In January 1901, the Mayhew store on "the point" burned to the ground, but the hotel was saved. This was a great loss for the Mayhews.[8] The hotel closed sometime after the fire, but was operating again in September 1902, with Mr. and Mrs. Ashford as managers.[9]

In 1903, Charlie Johnson purchased the Mayhew buildings, dock and property on the point. Mr. Johnson quickly began renovating the old Mayhew Hotel and reopened it in October 1903, with Mrs. Matt Lanktree as the hostess and manager.[10] Mr. Matt Lanktree also worked for Mr. Johnson from

Mayhew Hotel. *Circa 1894. (Photo Courtesy of Cook County Historical Society.)*

time to time. Under Johnson's ownership the name was changed to the Bay View Hotel. In the local paper it was also sometimes called the Lanktree Hotel[11] or the Langtry Hotel.[12] The name Langtry was a misspelling of Lanktree. The name Lanktree was used occasionally locally because businesses were sometimes identified by the manager's name instead of the actual business name. Sometime during the fall-winter of 1905-06 the hotel was damaged in a storm and had to be closed.[13] Mr. Johnson had it rebuilt and in April 1906 the Lanktree family moved back to the hotel from the logging camp on Maple Hill.[14] We know that the Bay View Hotel reopened that spring because the local paper reported that a Ladies Mission Society was scheduled to meet at the hotel in June. When the Bay View building quit functioning as a hotel is not certain.

In November 1906, Mrs. Matt Lanktree leased the Grand Hotel.[15] Earlier in the year, in August, Dr. F. B. Hicks had secured control of the old Mayhew residence and the adjoining six-room cottage and began converting them into a hospital.[16] Dr. Hick's hospital did not include the Mayhew's Hotel renamed the Bay View Hotel.[17] I found no evidence to indicate that Dr. Hicks had purchased the buildings from Charles Johnson, therefore, it must be assumed that some type rental or use arrangement was arrived at between the two men.

The Howenstine House

The other early lodging place during the later part of the 1800's was the "Howenstine House" on the west side of the bay.[18] When the house was built and when the Howenstine's started taking in guests is not clear. It is known that the building was dismantled in 1902.[19]

The Broadway Hotel

Due to the increasing demand for lodging in Grand Marais several new hotels or boarding houses were built in the years following the turn of the century. The first one built was the North Shore Hotel, later called the Broadway, on the northeast corner of Broadway and Wisconsin Street, where the Beaver House stands today. Like other hotels of the day this business was sometimes called by the owner's name. In this case the other name was the Larson Hotel.

Andrew Larson built the hotel in 1900, according to Rena Larson Eidnes, a daughter of Andrew Larson.[20] However, there was no announcement in the local newspaper about the hotel opening in 1900, but we do know it was open in 1901 because twenty members of the University of Minnesota football team came to Grand Marais in late August of 1901, for preseason practice and apparently stayed at the hotel.

In February,[21] April[22] and June of 1902,[23] there are references to a North Shore Hotel in the local paper, but no other information regarding the place was mentioned. Then on August 9, 1902, the local paper reports that: "The name of the local hotel has been changed from North Shore to Broadway. Landlord Larson has recently made a number of improvements to his house [hotel]

First advertisement for Broadway Hotel in *Cook County Herald*, August 9, 1902.

The second advertisement for the Broadway Hotel, August 23, 1902 in *Cook County Herald*. The same ad ran every week in the paper through January 24, 1903.

Broadway Hotel. *Circa 1905. (Photo courtesy of Cook County Historical Museum.)*

and is giving first class service,"[24] On the same date the first advertisement for the hotel is included in the paper. Consequently, it seems reasonable to speculate that the hotel may have been quite modest and in an unfinished stage during the first year or two when it was called the North Shore Hotel. When the building was finished a new name was selected and advertising of the hotel began.

The Leasing History of the Broadway

It appears that Mr. Larson never intended to personally manage or operate the hotel for long periods of time, because he leased out the building repeatedly during the first few years of ownership. It appears that the hotel was primarily an investment for Mr. Larson.

According to the local paper, the first person to lease the hotel was Mr. H. A. Gehrke,

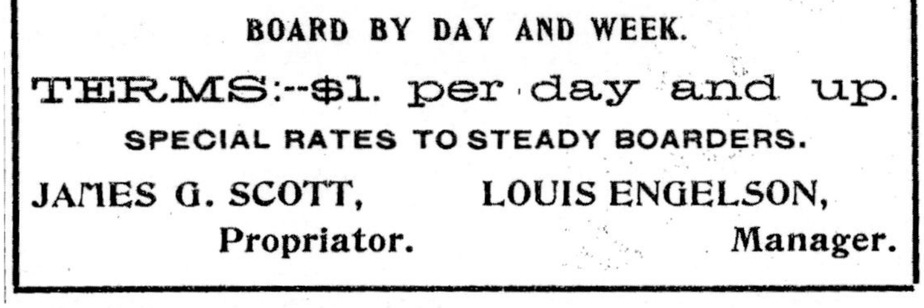

Advertisement in *Cook County Herald*, July 4, 1903. The same ad ran through September 19, 1903 in the paper.

Looking north on Broadway from Wisconsin Street. Broadway Hotel in foreground. The Fred Bramer Saloon is the first building to the left of the hotel. The Bramer building was located on lot 14, Block 31[25] *Circa 1905.* (Photo courtesy of *Cook County Historical Museum.*)

who in December 1902, leased the building for two years.[26] Less than a month later the paper announced that the hotel was closing for the winter "...on account of the inability of the proprietor to get the help necessary to carry on the business." [27] About five months later it was announced that Louis Engelson and James Scott had leased the hotel effective July 1, 1903.[28]

Approximately a year later the local paper reported that Fred R. Paine of Duluth had leased the Larson [Broadway] hotel.[29] In August of 1904, Mr. Paine began running the advertisement at the bottom of this page in the local paper.

In March of 1906, the hotel had a fire in a room that fortunately was extinguished before it became a serious fire. The incident was reported as follows:

> The careless handling of a lamp by a guest nearly caused a serious fire at the Broadway Tuesday evening. A cry of trouble was heard from the upper floor. The door was found to be locked and had to be broken in. The occupant of the room was found huddled in a corner behind the bed trying to protect himself from the smoke. He was dragged out half suffocated and attention was then turned to the fire, which was extinguished by the use of a few bucketfuls of water. The man had accidentally tipped over a lighted lamp, which was broken by the fall. The contents spilled over the floor and wall and became ignited, the flames spreading so quickly as to cut off escape for the bewildered

A FIRST CLASS HOTEL. NEW MANAGEMENT.

THE BROADWAY HOTEL.

FRED R. PAINE, Prop.

Headquarters for Tourists and Sportsmen.

RATES:
$1 and $1.50 a day. GRAND MARAIS, MINN.

Advertisement in *Cook County Herald*, August 13, 1904. This same ad ran every week for about two years.

guest and he retreated to the farthest corner and called for help.[30]

This is an excellent example of one of many fire risks that were associated with homes and businesses at the time.

In early July 1906, Mr. Paine ended his management of the Broadway Hotel with the intention of establishing his claim in Hovland as a place to accommodate hunters.[31] When the Paines left the Broadway, Ed Sterling took over the management of the hotel and continued in that position until the summer of 1909.[32]

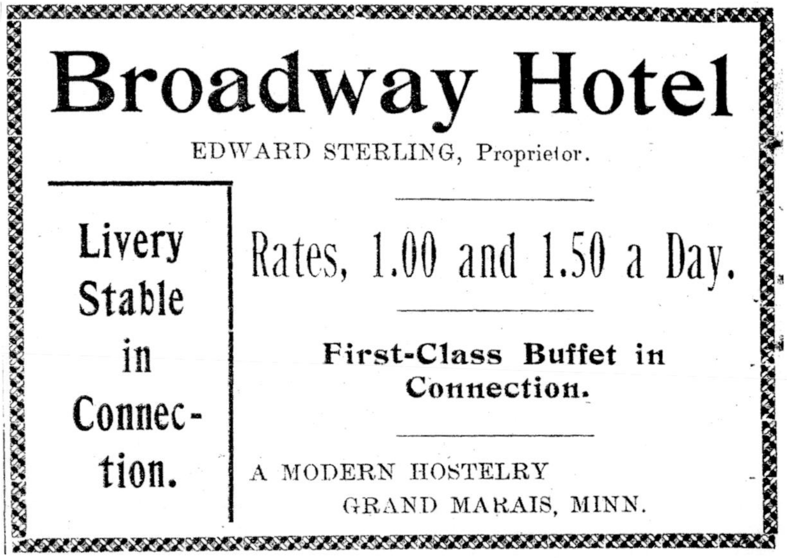

Advertisement in *Cook County News-Herald*, January 2, 1908. The same ad ran for several months.

The Paines returned to the area in October 1906 from a vacation and went to their property in Hovland and began making the place into the "Paine Ranch." The intent was to provide accommodations for big game hunters.[33] They did host several hunting parties in the fall, but this venture did not last long for the Paines.[34] In May of 1907, they moved to Toronto, Canada to work with his brother in a mining operation.[35]

During the summer of 1909, Andrew Larson took over the management of the Broadway Hotel again, until April 1, 1910, when he was able to rent the building to Mr. J. W. Babb.

Advertisement in *Cook County News-Herald*, August 19, 1909

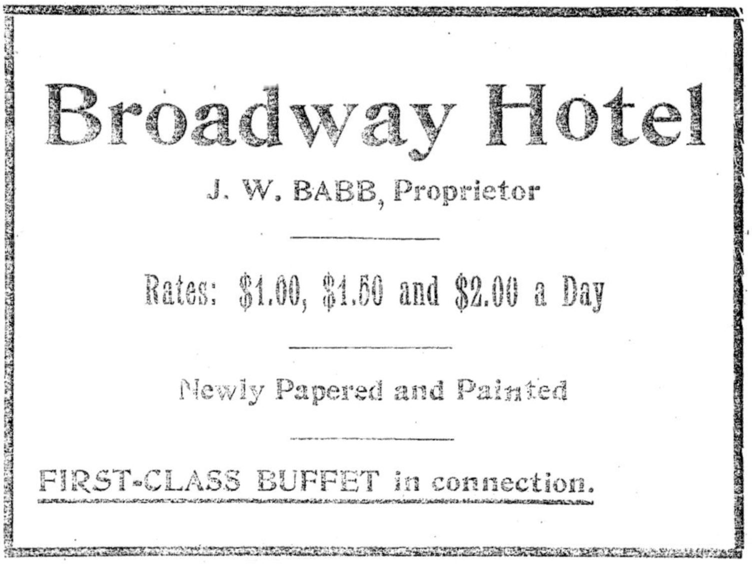

Advertisement in *Cook County News-Herald* by J. W. Babb, that ran from April 1910 through October 19, 1911.

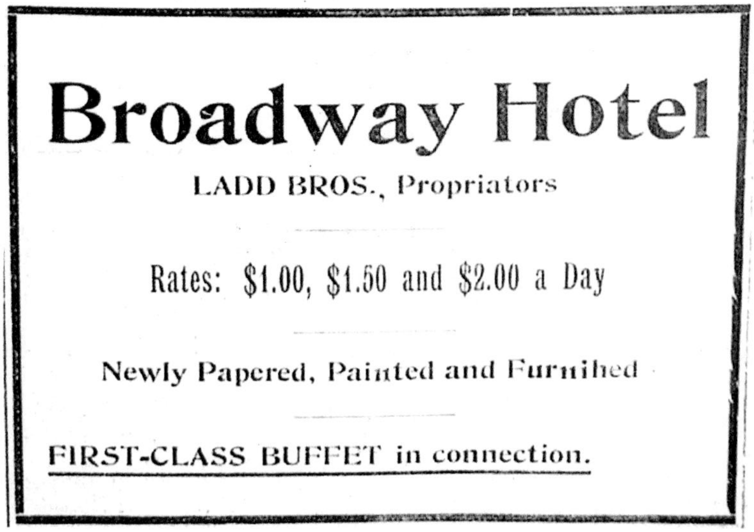

Advertisement in *Cook County News-Herald*, starting on October 26, 1911

On September 23, 1911, Mr. and Mrs. Andrew Larson sold the hotel to the Charles B. Ladd and Albert Ladd, who were brothers.[36] They ran the above advertisement weekly in the local paper until tragedy struck the town again in January 1913.

The Sterling Hotel

On September 3, 1910, Mrs. Belle Sterling purchased the western portion of lots 8, 9 and 10 from Mr. and Mrs. Andrew Jackson Scott.[37] The Scotts had built a house on the property in 1896, and it burned down about 1909.[38] The lots were near the east bay with lot 10 facing Wisconsin Street.[i] This is part of the property on which the East Bay Suites now stand. Soon after purchasing the property the Sterlings began building the Lake Side Hotel and Mrs. Sterling's Restaurant.[39] Mrs. Belle Sterling was soon left to own and manage the hotel and restaurant by herself due to the death of her husband, Edward, in July 1912.[40]

About six months after her husband's death Mrs. Sterling was struck with another loss when her hotel burned to the ground. At three a.m. on a Friday morning in late January 1913, a fire broke out in the Ashford Building on Broadway. By the time anyone had arrived on the scene the whole building was in flames. The fire quickly spread to the other businesses including the Broadway Hotel, Mrs. Belle Sterling's

[i] The parcel included in the western 66 feet of lot 10 and the westerly 93 feet of lots 8 and 9 in Block 46.

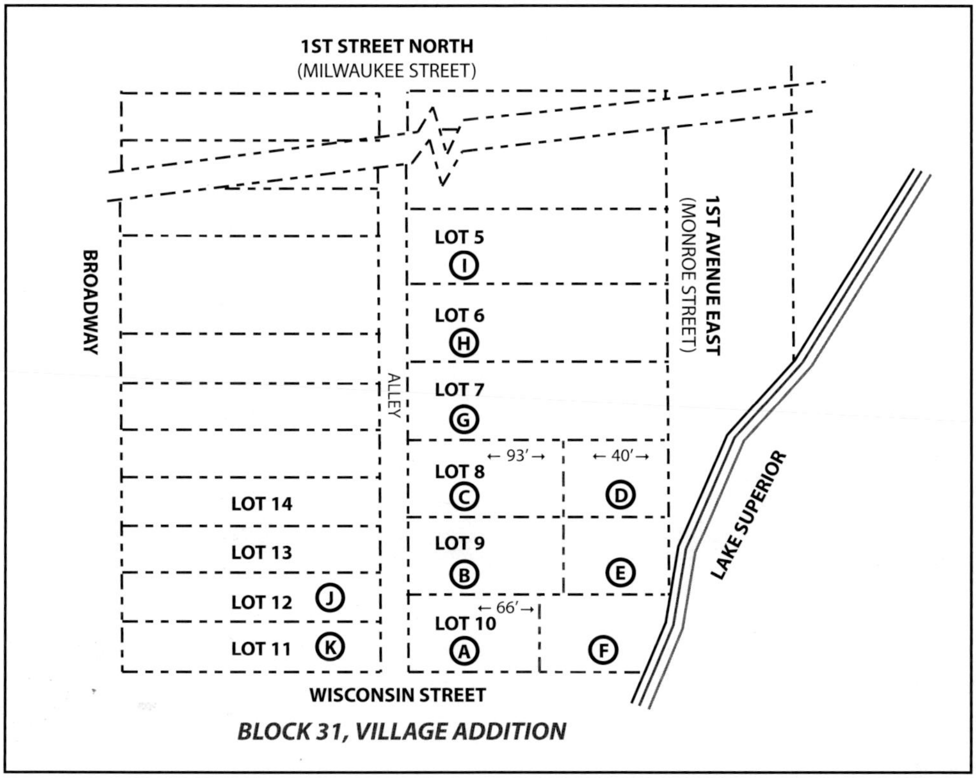

A partial map of Block 31 at the intersection of Wisconsin Street and Broadway. The blocks on the east half of the block are 40 feet wide and 25 feet wide on the west half of the block. *(Map drawn by Jim Ringquist.)*

Legend of Above Map

Parcels A, B, & C. Belle Sterling purchased from Mr. & Mrs. Andrew Jackson Scott on September 3, 1910.

Parcels D & E. Belle Sterling purchased from Mr.& Mrs. Louis Engelson on March 11, 1913. On October 10, 1901, Mr. and Mrs. Andrew Jackson Scott had sold these parcels to Charles J. Johnson. On August 8, 1904, Charles J. Johnson had sold the parcels, plus the **parcel labeled "F"** to the Johnson Mercantile Company. Later **lots D & E** were sold to the Engelsons. When Mrs. Sterling purchased the parcel labeled "**F**" is not certain.

Parcels **H & I**. **(Lots 5 & 6)** Belle Sterling purchased from Grand Marais State Bank on March 3, 1922. On April 1, 1913, a Tom McCormick had sold these lots to George Leng. Later they were obtained by the bank.

Lots **5, 6, 8, 9 & 10** were obtained by Mr. & Mrs. Sextus Lindahl from Belle Sterling on October 2, 1944. Mr. & Mrs. Lindahl sold to Mr. & Mrs. John Blackwell and Mr. & Mrs. Edward Dalbec on April 18, 1945. On October 16, 1945, Blackwells sold their 1/2 interest in the lots to the Dalbecs.

Parcel G Lot 7. On April 14, 1945, Mrs. & Mrs. John Blackwell purchased the lot from Mr. & Mrs. Sextus Lindahl. On August 17, 1945, Mr. & Mrs. Edward Dalbec purchased from Mr. & Mrs. Blackwell 1/2 interest in the parcel.

Lots 5,6,7,8,9 &10. Thelma Dalbec sold to Mr. and Mrs. James Pedersen on January 1, 1957.

Lots 11, 12 & 13 Mr. and Mrs. James Pedersen purchased these lots from Cook County Coop Store Association on November 27, 1962.

Lot 13 and the westerly 73 feet of lots 11 & 12. The Pedersens sold to Mr. & Mrs. William Cronberg on August 17, 1964.

Parcels A - K were sold by Mrs. Lois Pedersen, as East Bay Properties, LLC, in June 2005 to Gunflint Gals, LLC.

Boarding House, also called the Lake Side Hotel, Fred Winger's barber shop, Morris Johnson's pool hall, Stubstad & Company Dry Good Store and the Silas King Saloon. Some furniture was saved from the Broadway Hotel and Mrs. Sterling's Boarding House.[41]

Lake Side Hotel.[iii] *Circa 1913. (Photo courtesy Lois Pedersen Sundin.)*

The local paper reported, "A few of the victims were fairly well protected by insurance while in a couple of instances they had no insurance at all....Of the insured, Ladd Bros. are the heaviest losers. Owing to the extremely high insurance rate on their building they carried only about one-third of its real value, and consequently the loss falls pretty heavily on them."[42]

It is understandable that insurance rates would be very high on frame buildings built close together in small rural towns. The history of such buildings being destroyed by fires during this period would make any insurance company apprehensive about their risks.

This was the end of the Broadway Hotel, but Mrs. Sterling soon made plans to rebuild her hotel. On March 11, 1913, she purchased additional land adjacent to her original property. This included the easterly 40 feet of lots 8 & 9 from Mr. and Mrs. Louis Engelson.[43] This extended her property to the bay where these lots were located.[ii] She had the foundation completed by mid-May 1913.[44]

[ii] Charles J. Johnson has purchased these two parcels from Mr. and Mrs. Andrew Jackson Scott in October 1901. Book I, Deed Record, p. 35, Recorders Office, Cook County Court House, Grand Marais, MN.

[iii] The sign at the top of the building reads Lake Side Hotel, and the sign on the porch roof reads Restaurant Mrs. Sterling. The identity of the people in the picture is unknown. After considerable research regarding the Sterling's Hotel, I was fairly certain that the building in the above photo was the Lake Side Hotel that burned in 1913. But after discovering a photo of Wisconsin Street taken during the summer of 1917, with a partial view of the Lake Side Hotel in the background, it now seems reasonable to conclude that the above photo is the building Mrs. Sterling had constructed after the fire in 1913. If the above photo is a picture of the Sterling's hotel, which was built in 1910, and burned in January 1913, then the second hotel was similar in appearance to the earlier hotel. Because Mrs. Sterling began rebuilding the second hotel quickly after the fire, it is possible that the two buildings were identical.

A few years later on March 3, 1922, Mrs. Sterling purchased lots 5 and 6 north of her current lots. However, she never did own lot 7, which was located between her original hotel site and lots 5 and 6. In late 1922, Mrs. Sterling began construction of a large addition to the hotel, which included 26 rooms.[45] When the name of the hotel was changed to Sterling Hotel is unclear. We do know that it was called the Sterling after the addition was completed in 1923. There were no advertisements for the hotel in the local papers between 1913 and 1922 to help indicate when the name was changed.

From photographs of the hotel it appears that Mrs. Sterling added another addition or additions to the back of the hotel between the late-twenties and/or late-thirties. Although documentation for the dates of one or more addition is not available, it does seem reasonable to assume that an addition could have been added in the late-twenties, before the depression or after the depression between1935 and 1940. However, it is hard to believe that Mrs. Sterling would have made an addition to the hotel in the late thirties when she was about 64 years of age.

Nevertheless, there are at least two arguments for supporting the later date for an addition. One argument is the fact that the Tourist Hotel had burned down in January 1931 and there may have been a need for additional hotel rooms in Grand Marais, when the country was emerging from the depression and tourism was increasing in Grand Marais. The second argument for the later date for the additions is the report that Mrs. Sterling had lost the property through foreclosure to Sextus Lindahl in 1944. This information was included in a report of Mrs. Sterling's death, in the local newspaper in March 1945.[46] From a Certificate of Title document we do know that Sextus Lindahl was the owner of the property as of October 2, 1944.[47] It is safe to assume that the hotel business was down in the early forties due to World War II. This could have created financial problems for Mrs. Sterling that resulted in making it difficult to make payments on loans she may have taken out to finance an addition to the hotel in the late thirties or in 1940.

Whatever was involved in the transfer or sale of the hotel to Sextus Lindahl, it is clear that Mrs. Sterling operated a successful hotel/restaurant business for about thirty-four years. When she died she was enroute to visit her sister and brother in Newburg, Ontario, Canada. While enroute "Mrs. Sterling became ill on the bus and the driver advised her to get off at Manistique [Michigan] and get a room at a lodging house there. During the night another guest in the next room heard groans coming from the one occupied by Mrs. Sterling and upon investigation found Mrs. Sterling in a state of comma. She was rushed to the hospital, but she died shortly thereafter."[48] At the time of her death she was at least 70 years old.

Postcard photo of Sterling Hotel. *Circa 1923. (Postcard courtesy Lois Pedersen Sundin.)*

The Sterling Hotel. *Circa late 1920's. (Photo courtesy of Lois Pedersen Sundin.)*

Postcard of Sterling Hotel. Note the addition to the back of the Hotel. *Circa 1940. (Postcard courtesy of Bill and Beth Blank.)*

Postcard of East Bay Hotel. *Circa 1950's. (Postcard courtesy of Bill and Beth Blank.)*

The East Bay Hotel

Mr. Lindahl owned the property for just a little more than six months before selling it to Mr. and Mrs. (Selma) John Blackwell and Mr. and Mrs. (Thelma) Edward Dalbec as equal owners on April 18, 1945.[49] They changed the name of the place to the East Bay Hotel.

At the time Ed Dalbec was a game warden in Cook County, a position he resigned from in January 1947.[50] Mr. and Mrs. Dalbec managed the hotel following the purchase and during the summer of 1945, Arvid and Amy Nelsen were hired to manage the restaurant for the new owners.

The Nelsen family lived in an apartment in the hotel that later was remodeled into the Viking Lounge. At the end of the summer tourist season in 1945, the Nelsens moved to the Soderberg building and shortly after that Amy Hussey began managing the restaurant.[51] She held this position a few years, perhaps until 1953, when she and her husband purchased Naniboujou Lodge.

Prior to the above transaction Mr. and Mrs. John Blackwell had owned lot 7, which was the parcel that was located between lots 6 and 8 in the above-mentioned transaction. On August 17, 1945, the Blackwells sold lot 7[52] to Mr. and Mrs. Edward Dalbec and two months later on October 16, 1945, sold their interest in the hotel property to them also.[53]

During the summer of 1947, the Dalbec's only child, Loren, was drowned in an airplane accident in the entrance area of the Grand Marais Harbor. This was a terrible blow to Mr. and Mrs. Dalbec. Because the Dalbecs had purchased the hotel with some thought about the possibility of Loren taking over the business, his death had major ramifications for the Dalbecs. Mr. Dalbec soon lost interest in the business and he and Thelma moved to the State of Oregon in the fall of 1947 or in 1948.

Prior to moving they hired Mr. and Mrs. (Lena) Jim Pedersen to manage the hotel and restaurant for them. Lena had worked for the Dalbecs on and off prior to being hired, with her husband, to manage the business, so she had some knowledge of the

Postcard photo of East Bay Dinning Room. *Circa 1960. (Postcard courtesy of Lois Pedersen Sundin.)*

East Bay Hotel. *Circa 1980's.(Photo courtesy of Lois Pedersen Sundin.)*

business. Earlier Jim and Lena had moved to the Grand Marais area when they purchased what was called the Green Door Cabins in Croftville.

Jim and Lena Pedersen ran the business until December 15, 1956, when their son Jim "Pete" and his wife Lois began managing the business due to the failing health of Jim Sr. Earlier Jim Sr. had been diagnosed with cancer and had told his son, Jim "Pete" and Lois that he thought Thelma Dalbec wanted to sell the property. This led to the sale of the hotel on January 1, 1957, to Jim "Pete" and Lois Pedersen. At the time Thelma Dalbec was living in Salem, Oregon.[54] Ed Dalbec had died in the early fifties, thus leaving Thelma as a widow at the time of the sale.

Lois Pedersen was the daughter of Mr. and Mrs. Val Dalbec and niece of Ed and Thelma Dalbec. She and Jim "Pete" had worked in the hotel various times during their high school and college years. Jim "Pete" Pedersen had graduated from Cook County High School in 1947, and Lois Dalbec in 1948. Following high school Jim attended the University of Minnesota-Duluth, and Lois attended Gustavus Adolphus College and the University of Minnesota, from which she graduated in 1952. Following graduation Lois taught school for two years. Jim's education was interrupted when he was drafted into the military during the Korean War. After he returned from the service he graduated from the University of Minnesota-Duluth in 1954. Jim and Lois, who had been friends since high school days, were united in marriage in June 1954.[55]

A Portion of Wisconsin Street. Left to Right: Leng's Fountain, The Market, The Coop Store and Pioneer House on the right. Aftermath of November 1960 storm. *(Photo courtesy of Cook County Historical Society.)*

The CO-OP Store and Beaver House Connection

On November 27, 1962, the Pedersens purchased the building and three lots on the corner of Wisconsin and Broadway from the Cook County Cooperative Store Association.[55] The CO-OP Store had been closed since October 1960.[56] This is the same corner on which the Broadway Hotel once stood.[iv]

The primary reason the Pedersens purchased the lots was to add parking space for their hotel and restaurant guests. When the CO-OP owned the property the back part of the store was a storage area for grain and other products that were sold to area residents. The Pedersens had that part of the building torn down to create the parking lot they needed and put up for sale the westerly part of lots 11 and 12 on which the building was located and the adjacent lot 13 to the north.

On August 17, 1964, the Pedersens sold one-half interest in the property to Mr. and Mrs. (Betty) William Cronberg,[57] and one-half interest in the property to Mr. and Mrs. (Gladys) Guyal Anderson.[58] The Cronbergs converted the building into the Beaver House, a bait and tackle supply store and in 1976 purchased the Anderson's interest in the property.[59]

Pedersens Sell the East Bay Hotel

In a brochure about the business printed in the late 1970's or 1980's, Lois wrote as follows about the East Bay Hotel:

"We have tried to keep the feel of the old Hotel, and yet modernize as required to keep the place comfy and cozy. The building is old - yet has a certain dignity. We hope you will ignore the squeaking, uneven floors; the occasional new roof leaks; the now and then

East end of Wisconsin Street. Note the back part of the CO-OP Store, which was torn down by the Pedersens. 1951. *(The photo is a portion of a larger photo courtesy of Lois Pedersen Sundin.)*

Bottom to Top on left side of street: Alm's Store, a Bar, Jackson's Cafe & Bus Depot, Humphrey's Clothing and Photo Art Shop, C.O. Backlund Hardware, Leng's Fountain, Leng's Market, CO-OP and East Bay Hotel. Bottom to top on right side of street: Tony's Lunch, Shore Theater, a small shop that housed various businesses over the years, Toftey's Store, and Pioneer House. To the right of the Pioneer House is the current Cook County Historical Society Museum, and to the right of that is the site of the current Shoreline Motel.

The Beaver House. *2008.*

plumbing difficulties; and the lack of space in the guest rooms. In this day of large, modern motel rooms we feel it is a unique experience to stay in an old hotel with all that character and history. We hope you will find it enjoyable and come back often as many of our guests do."

Jim and Lois managed the hotel and restaurant until the early 1990's, when they turned the management of the business over to their sons David and Mark. During their management period, a large addition was added to the north end of the hotel.

On April 15, 2000, Jim Pedersen died and Lois became the sole owner. On September 25, 2003, Lois put the property into a corporate entity called East Bay Properties, LLC, and in June 2005 sold the hotel to Teresa Sterns and Jane Helmke of Gunflint Gals, LLC.[61] The new owners demolished older portions of the hotel and renovated the wing built during the 1990's, converting the entire building into vacation condominiums. As part of this major change to an old Grand Marais landmark they changed the name to East Bay Suites.

The Gunflint Gals, LLC sold their interest in the East Bay Suites property to the East Bay Suites Condominium Association in 2009. Following this transaction the association signed a contract with Odyssey Development to begin managing the property on November 1, 2009.

The new East Bay Suites viewed from Wisconsin Street. *September 2008*

(Endnotes)

1. F. B. Hicks, "Historian Tells of Early Beginnings of Grand Marais as an Indian Trading Post," *Duluth News Tribune,* October 6, 1929, p. 12.

2. Steven J. Wright, "Thomas Mayhew: Common Pioneer, Unique Man." Duluth News Tribune, Outlook Section, February 4, 1979, p. 74.

3. "An Old Landmark Destroyed by Fire," *Cook County News-Herald*, October 11, 1916, p. 1.

4. "LOCAL PICK-UPS," *Cook County Herald*, JULY 22, 1899, p. 3.

5. Willis H. Raff *Pioneers in the Wilderness* (Grand Marais, MN: Cook County Historical Society, 1981), p. 48.

6. Willis H. Raff, *Pioneers in the Wilderness* (Grand Marais, MN: Cook County Historical Society, 1981), p.58.

7. "LOCAL PICK-UPS," *Cook County Herald*, September 23, 1899, p. 3.

8. *Cook County Herald*, January 19, 1901.

9. "Caught on the Run," *Cook County Herald*, September 27, 1902, p. 5.

10. Willis H. Raff, *Pioneers in the Wilderness* (Grand Marais, MN: Cook County Historical Society, 1981), p. 353.

11. "Topics of a Week," *Cook County Herald*, June 2, 1906, p. 5.

12. *Cook County Herald*, April 23, 1904, p. 3.

13. Willis H. Raff, *Pioneers in the Wilderness* (Grand Marais, MN: Cook County Historical Society, 1981), p. 368.

14. Topics of a Week," *Cook County Herald*, April 21, 1906, p. 3.

15. Topics of a Week," *Cook County Herald*, November 3, 1906, p. 3.

16. "A New Hospital," *Cook County Herald*, August 4, 1906, p. 5.

17. "An Old Landmark Destroyed by Fire," *Cook County News-Herald*, October 11, 1916, p. 1.

18. Willis H. Raff, *Pioneers in the Wilderness* (Grand Marais, MN: Cook County Historical Society, 1981), p. 48.

19. "Caught on the Run," *Cook County Herald*, February 8, 1902, p. 3.

20. "Jots By Ade...Rena Eidnes Recalls Village of Grand Marais In 1897." *Cook County News-Herald*, April 18, 1974, p. 4.

21. "Caught on the Run," *Cook County Herald*, February 1, 1902, p. 3.

22. "Caught on the Run," *Cook County Herald*, April 19, 1902, 1902, p. 3.

23. "Caught on the Run," *Cook County Herald*, June 21, 1902, 1902, p. 5.

24. "Caught on the Run," *Cook County Herald*, August 9, 1902, p. 5.

25. "Caught on the Run," *Cook County Herald*, June 6, 1903. p. 5.

26. "Caught on the Run," *Cook County Herald*, December 27, 1902, p. 3.

27. "Caught on the Run," *Cook County Herald*, January 24, 1903, p. 3.

28. "Caught on the Run," *Cook County Herald*, July 4, 1903, p. 5.

29. "LOCAL ITEMS." *Cook County Herald*, June 4, 1904, p. 5.

30. *Cook County Herald*, March 10, 1906, p.35.

31. "Topics of a Week," *Cook County Herald*, June 9, 1906, p. 3.

32. "Topics of a Week," *Cook County Herald*, July 17, 1906, p. 3.

33. "Topics of a Week," *Cook County Herald*, October 13, 1906, p. 5.

34. "Topics of a Week," *Cook County Herald*, October 27, 1906, p. 3.

35. "Topics of a Week," *Cook County Herald*, April 27, 1907, p. 3.

36. Book R, Warranty Deed Record, p. 203, Recorders Office, Cook County Court House, Grand Marais, MN.

37. Book R, Deed Record, p. 122, Recorders Office, Cook County Court House, Grand Marais, MN.

38. Willis H. Raff, *Pioneers in the Wilderness* (Grand Marais, MN: Cook County Historical Society, 1981), p. 27.

39. Willis H. Raff, *Pioneers in the Wilderness* (Grand Marais, MN: Cook County Historical Society, 1981), p. 27.

40. "Death of Ed Sterling," *Cook County Herald*, July 11, 1912, p. 1.

41. "FIRE-SWEPT AGAIN," *Cook County News-Herald*, January 30, 1913, p.1.

42. "FIRE-SWEPT AGAIN," *Cook County News-Herald*, January 30, 1913, p.1.

43. Book R, Deed Record, pp. 200 & 328, Recorders Office, Cook County Court House, Grand Marais, MN.

44. "Topics of a Week," *Cook County News-Herald*, May 15, 1913, p. 1.

45. "News-ettes of Grand Marais and Vicinity," *Cook County News-Herald*, November 23, 1922, p. 4.

46. Mrs. B. C. Sterling Dies on Way to Canada, *Cook County News-Herald*, March 22, 1945, p. 1.

47. Book 10, Certificate of Titles, p. 66, Document # 2693. Recorders Office, Cook County Court House, Grand Marais, MN.

48. Mrs. B. C. Sterling Dies on Way to Canada, *Cook County News-Herald*, March 22, 1945, p. 1.

49. Book 10, Certificate of Titles, p. 93, Document # 2720, Recorders Office, Cook County Court House, Grand Marais, MN.

50. "Ed. Dalbec Resigns as Game Warden Here," *Cook County News-Herald*, January 9, 1947, p. 1.

51. Interview with Roger Nelsen, April 3, 2008

52. Book 4, Quit Claim Deeds Record, p. 249, Recorders Office, Cook County Court House, Grand Marais, MN.

53. Book 10, Certificate of Titles, p. 111, Document # 2737, Recorders Office, Cook County Court House, Grand Marais, MN.

54. Book 54, Warranty Deeds, pp. 265 & 266, Recorders Office, Cook County Court House, Grand Marais, MN.

55. "Lois Dalbec and James Peterson Wed," *Cook County News-Herald*, July 1, 1954, p. 1.

56. Book 28, Deed Record, p. 327, Recorders Office, Cook County Court House, Grand Marais, MN.

57. Advertisement. "Closing Out Sale Cook County CO-OP Store," *Cook County News-Herald*, October 15, 1960, p. 5.

58. Book 31, Deed Record, p. 102, Recorders Office, Cook County Court House, Grand Marais, MN.

59. Book 31, Deed Record, p. 101, Recorders Office, Cook County Court House, Grand Marais, MN.

60. Book 48, Deed Record, p. 434, Recorders Office, Cook County Court House, Grand Marais, MN.

61. Book 28, Certificates of Titles, p. 49, Document # 9227, Recorders Office, Cook County Court House, Grand Marais, MN.

Chapter 5

The Grand Hotel and P. E. Alm Store

The Grand Hotel

In December 1902, John Leonard Lundin purchased the lot located on the northeast corner of First Avenue West and Wisconsin Street from the Grand Marais Realty and Improvement Company. This is the parcel where Joynes parking lot is now located.

The Grand Hotel. *Circa 1905. (Photo courtesy of Cook County Historical Museum.)*

Soon after purchasing the lot John Lundin began erecting a building on it.[1]

In January 1903, it was reported that the building was a two-story structure 48 x 50 feet and that the first floor was to be used for a store and the upper story for a public hall.[2] On June 6, 1903, the local paper reported that Gust Olson had rented the building from Mr. Lundin and he planned to "...conduct a saloon in one room and a restaurant in the other room on the first floor, while the second floor will be devoted to lodging rooms."[3] Less than a month later the hotel, now called the Grand, was taking in guests. The need for another hotel is evident from the following paragraph in the local paper:

> The Broadway, filled to overflowing, turned many away, who, with others, in anticipation of the rush there, proceeded

to the new hotel, whose name we understand is 'The Grand', and filled that also. It is evident that further improvements must be made at once to meet the demands of the traveling public. Our fast growing village is rapidly gaining in importance and

First advertisement of the Grand Hotel in the *Cook County Herald* on July 4, 1903. This ad ran weekly for several months.

distinction and must meet the requirements that prosperity thrust upon it.[4]

After a few months with no advertisements in the local paper, a smaller ad was run several times.

Advertisement in *Cook County Herald* on May 21, 1904.

On June 4, 1904, the local paper reported that Gust Olson had transferred his hotel and saloon business to Jacob H. Carlson, who was to take charge as soon a he had secured a license for which he had applied.[5] This deal either fell through, or Mr. Carlson decided to get out of the business because in November of the same year Ed Sterling rented the Grand Hotel from Gust Olson.[6]

About six months later, in late April or early May, Gust Olson was forced to sell all the stock of liquor, the furniture and fixtures in the saloon and hotel owned by him at a sale conducted by the local Sheriff. The prices at which items sold were very low and gave Mr. Olson a very small margin over the amount owed his creditors. The news article about the sale continued with the following comments:

Mr. Olson is entitled to and shares the sympathy of the public. His financial

> difficulties were accelerated by troubles of a far more serious nature. For a long time he has been handicapped in his business operation by failing eyesight, for which he has been unable to obtain relief. Driven from business, with property sacrificed – these misfortunes are as nothing compared with almost total blindness, with which he is now afflicted. Once prosperous in a business way and prominent in local politics, active in public affairs, enjoying the blessings of perfect physical manhood – now reduced to a state of helplessness, Mr. Olson's predicament is surely enough to excite feeling of sympathy in a heart of stone.[7]

Sometime after Gust Olson's sale of his furnishings and the supplies in the Grand Hotel, Mr. Lundin apparently hired a Mr. Joe Mason as interim manager of the building. This assumption is based on the following report in the *Cook County Herald* on October 12, 1905.

> C. K. Grewar has succeeded Joe Mason as manager of the Grand Hotel, the transfer having been made early this week. The hotel is being thoroughly renovated throughout and the management is prepared to offer first class accommodations to the hotel trade. Mr. Grewar has moved his barbershop into the hotel building. Mr. Mason has accepted a position as cook in a neighboring lumber camp during the winter.[8]

Approximately six months later, on April 7, 1906, it was announced that John Johnson of Tofte had "...leased the saloon and hotel property of J. L. Lundin, succeeding C. K. Grewar in the management of same."[9] Two weeks later it was announced that Mr. and Mrs. Dick Russell had taken charge of the Grand Hotel.[10] Apparently John Johnson had hired the Russells to manage the hotel for him. Approximately six months later, on October 20, 1906, the local paper

---

Under New Management. **CarefulS ervice.**

GRAND HOTEL,

C. K. GREWAR, Prop.

The leading hotel. The Popular place fot dinner parties.

Excellent Table Service.
Clean, bright and comfortable rooms.

Grand Marais, Minn

Advertisement in Cook County Herald, January 6, 1906.

Grand Hotel,

JOHN JOHNSON, Prop.

Clean and comfortable rooms. Table service the best the market affords. Rates reasonable. Stable in connection.

Johnson's Buffet

is run on business principles. No "hangers on;" no rowdyism. Our stock is most complete. Our patrons get what they call for in—

Wines, Liquors, Cigars.

Advertisement in the *Cook County Herald* on November 9, 1907. Johnson ran this ad weekly through June 8, 1908.

reported that, "Mrs. Richard Russell, who has successfully conducted the Grand hotel [sic] during the past summer has retired from the business. The business will be continued by John Johnson, lessee of the property."[11]

Fire Destroys the Grand Hotel and Other Buildings

On October 12, 1908, tragedy struck the town of Grand Marais. A fire started in the Grand Marais Mercantile Company store and spread to the Grand Hotel, Cook County State Bank, and Charles J. Johnson's residence. All were destroyed by the fire. The building to the right of the Grand Hotel in the picture below was not mentioned in the report of the fire, but presumably it was also destroyed. The Broadway Hotel which was located across the street from the Grand Marais Mechantile Company was saved by "...water being constantly thrown against

Wisconsin Street. Left to right: Grand Hotel, uncertain of name of building or business, Charlie Johnson's Grand Marais Mercantile Company and the Cook County State Bank. The building in the far right is the Broadway Hotel. *Circa 1905.* (Photo courtesy of Cook County Historical Society.)

the side of the building to keep it from igniting."[12]

Whether the Cook County State Bank or the Mercantile Company was facing Wisconsin Street or Broadway at the time is not clear.

Charlie Johnson had built the store on the corner in 1901 on lots he had purchased on February 26, 1898, from Edward W. Wakelin.[13] On August 8, 1904, Johnson transferred these lots, plus several others to a corporation called Johnson Mercantile Company. In 1905, Johnson sold the store to C. H. Taylor, who in 1907 brought in other investors and incorporated the business with the name Grand Marais Mercantile Company.[14]

Regarding the location of the store, Bill Raff states, "According to Charlie's brother, it was on Broadway, facing the Lake, near the intersection of Wisconsin Street, 'where the Leng building is now.' Van (Charlie's brother) recalled, too, that it was set off by a 'nice flower garden'"[15]

This description implies that there was space in front of the building facing Broadway. It seems reasonable to assume that this garden area in front of the store became the location of the building that first housed the Cook County State Bank. From the picture on page 82, it also appears that the bank building fronted on Wisconsin Street and the entrance to Johnson's store was switched to face Wisconsin Street.

The location of Charlie Johnson's residence that was destroyed in the fire is also a bit of a mystery. It is known that in June 1903, Johnson purchased a new residence on the East Bay, east of the Broadway Hotel.[16] Less than a year later, in April 1904, Johnson purchased the John A. Miller property on the bay front and had made plans to remodel and improve the building for residence purposes.[17] The April 16, 1904, edition of the local paper reported that he was preparing to move into his new residence.

In addition, he was "fitting his old residence for office purposes" and the Village Council had decided to rent rooms in this house for office space. Exactly where these houses were located, I have not been able to determine. Since the first residence was east of the Broadway Hotel and the other one was on the bay front it seems unreasonable to assume that one of these houses was the residence that burned down. However, it is possible that the wind blew embers to one of the houses causing it to be burned. It also is possible that the residence referred to in the report of the fire was the apartment that Charlie earlier had in the back of the store.

The P. E. Alm General Merchandise Store

John Lundin soon replaced the hotel building with a new one-story structure that was to last for about 70 years. The building was built with wood and faced with brick. Lundin leased the building out to various businessmen until he sold it to Peter Alm in 1915. The following account about the various businesses in the building was compiled from the recollections of Cac Hussy, John Blackwell, Lois Osgood, M. J. Humphrey,

Ade and Bertha Toftey and Howard Joynes and published in the *Cook County News-Herald* in April 23, 1981.

During its early years the building was frequently split into various business. "In its beginning, the east half of the building was a grocery store run by John W. Badb [sic] (Babb) and Lever H. Lien. The west half was split in two and Peter Alm had the furthest west end portion. The center quarter of the building was operated by Dr. F. H. Hicks and Carrie Scott.

Peter Alm's name was to be remembered as having had dry goods for the longest period of time and it was his ownership and longevity in the building that was outstanding.

In Pete's Dry Goods store, you could buy some of the best lines it is said, such as Pendleton, Woolrich and the like. The Forest Service was later dressed in uniforms from his store and Pete carried everything from head to toe. If you felt like making a gingham dress, chances are Pete had the yard goods and the thread.

Postcard of P. E. Alm Store where Grand Hotel stood and Joynes' Parking Lot is now located. *Circa 1935. (Photo by Milford Humphrey, Postcard courtesy of Lois Pedersen Sundin.)*

Ed Toftey, Ade Toftey's brother, came to Grand Marais to run a grocery business after fire gutted his Tofte saw mill in 1910. The mill was said to have hired about 25 men and was a substantial business, but Ed was burned out.

Ed bought into the corner building, buying Badb [sic] and Lien out. It was in the early spring [1910] that Ed joined Pete in the building, forming a separate grocery business complimentary to Pete's goods.[18]

Photo of Wisconsin Street in 1934. Buses and trucks in the photo are for transporting CCC workers to camps. The Soderberg Store (Shore View Hotel) is the two-story building in the middle of the photo. The building to the right of the Soderberg building is an old livery stable. P. E. Alms store is the building with the awning next to the Shore View Hotel. Photo by M. J. Humphrey. *(Photo courtesy of Cook County Historical Society.)*

In the spring of 1913, Ed Toftey built a store of his own, on the southwest corner of Broadway and Wisconsin Street, the current location of the Security State Bank.[19] He moved into the new building in late July of the same year.[20] The new business was called the Ed Toftey Company and sold groceries and hardware. It also had the first gas pump in town. When Ed Tofte left Pete Alm's building, J. Blackwell put furniture in the east side of the building."[21]

After John L. Lundin died, Peter E. Alm purchased the building and land for $1,700, on June 28, 1915, with William Carlson and Fred Jackson serving as executors of Lundin's estate. The land on which the building was located included two lots, seventy-five feet long and approximately twenty-five feet wide at the corner of Wisconsin Street and First Avenue West.[22] On September 14, 1925, Peter Alm purchased an additional forty-five feet of land north of the original two lots he had purchased in 1915.[23]

Joynes Department Store

In 1941, Howard and Rosemary Joynes bought the business and leased the building from Pete Alm when he retired. When Joynes became the proprietor he arranged for the store to become a member of the Federated Store chain based in Chicago and Minneapolis. Joynes continued to lease the store from Pete Alm[i] or his daughter Lois Osgood for many years.[24] On June 20, 1953,

Joynes Federated Store. *Circa 1948. (Photo courtesy of Cook County Historical Museum.)*

Howard and Rosemary Joynes signed a new lease for the building with Lois Osgood and Lynden Osgood. This lease was for five years and renewable with an option to purchase the building and lot.[25] In the fall of 1953, Joynes began construction of a new store, across the street from his Federated Store on the northwest corner of First Avenue West and Wisconsin Street.[26] This store opened in May 1954 with the west portion of the store being a Ben Franklin Store and the east side Joynes Department Store.[27]

In 2006, Howard celebrated 65 years of successful business on the corner of Wisconsin and First Street. His granddaughter Julie Carlson currently manages the business.

Joynes Ben Franklin. In the right side of the picture is the Soderberg building that was moved from the corner of 1st Ave. W. and Wisconsin Street. *Summer 2007*

---

[i] Peter Alm passed away in September 1951

The Joynes Parking lot. Summer 2007

Howard on the right, Rosemary his wife in the middle and their son Dick on the left. Dick and Rosemary worked in the store for years and are now both deceased. Photo taken in 1963. *(Courtesy of Cook County News-Herald.)*

Howard Joynes, age 90 and granddaughter Julie Joynes Carlson. March 8, 2008.

After opening their new store, Howard and Rosemary Joynes used the old Federated Store building for storage and a type of discount store called the Bargain Barn for many years. The Bargain Barn was open only in the summers and sometimes for only short periods of time. Howard and Rosemary Joynes remained as either leaseholders or in some stage of purchasing the property until December 5, 1979, when a judge ruled that they be awarded clear title to the Old Federated Store building and the two lots ninety feet in length from Wisconsin Street.[28]

The Donut Shop also rented space in the old Federated Building from 1969 to 1978. In 1981, Howard Joynes had the old Federated Store building demolished and he converted the space into a parking lot for his customers. At that time the Blue Water Cafe worked out an agreement with Howard to rent space on the parking lot sign so its customers could also use the parking lot.

(Endnotes)

1. "CAUGHT ON THE RUN." *Cook County Herald*, December 27, 1902, p. 3.

2. "CAUGHT ON THE RUN." *Cook County Herald*, January 24, 1903, p. 3.

3. "CAUGHT ON THE RUN." *Cook County Herald*, June 6, 1903, p. 5.

4. "CAUGHT ON THE RUN." *Cook County Herald*, June 27, 1903, p. 5.

5. 'LOCAL ITEMS," *Cook County Herald*, June 4, 1904, p. 5.

6. "Topics of a Week," *Cook County Herald*, November 12, 1904, p 5.

7. "Topics of a Week," *Cook County Herald*, May 6, 1905, .

8. "Topics of a Week," *Cook County Herald*, October 12, 1905, p.5.

9. "Topics of a Week," *Cook County Herald*, April 7, 1906, p.3.

10. "Topics of a Week," *Cook County Herald*, April 21, 1906, p.3 .

11. "Topics of a Week," *Cook County Herald*, October 20, 1906, p.5.

12. "$50,000 FIRE MONDAY," *Cook County News-Herald*, October 15, 1908, P. 1

13. Book E, Deed Record, p. 164, Recorders Office, Cook County Court House, Grand Marais, MN.

14. "Topics of A Week," *Cook County Herald*, March 30, 1907, p. 3.

15. Willis H. Raff, *Pioneers in the Wilderness* (Grand Marais, MN: Cook County Historical Society, 1981), p. 349.

16. "CAUGHT ON THE RUN." *Cook County Herald*, June 20, 1903, p. 5.

17. 'LOCAL ITEMS," *Cook County Herald*, April 9, 1904, p. 3.

18. "Build's 80-Year History Brought to A Close," *Cook County News-Herald*, April 23, 1981, p.1.

19. "Topics of a Week," *Cook County News-Herald*, July 7, 1913, p. 1

20. "Topics of a Week," *Cook County News-Herald*, July 31, 1913, p. 1

21. "Build's 80-Year History Brought to A Close," *Cook County News-Herald*, April 23, 1981, p.1.

22. Book W, Deed Record, p. 1, Recorders Office, Cook County Court House, Grand Marais, MN.

23. Book 2, Quit Claim Deed Record, p. 144, Recorders Office, Cook County Court House, Grand Marais, MN.

24. "Past-Plus...and Present," *Cook County News-Herald*, May 6, 1954, p. 2.

25. Book 22, Miscellaneous Record, p 21, Cook County Recorders Office, Grand Marais, MN.

26. "Joynes to Open Store in '54," *Cook County News-Herald*, December 31,1953, p.1.

27. "New Joynes Store Has Big Opening," *Cook County News-Herald*, May 13, 1954, p. 1.

28. Book 67, Mortgage Record, p. 410, Judgment, December 4, 1979, Recorders Office, Cook County Court House, Grand Marais, MN.

Chapter 6

The Soderberg and Humphrey Buildings

Johnson's New Place

On July 10, 1906, John Johnson purchased two lots, numbers 12 and 13 in block 20, on the northwest corner of First Avenue West and Wisconsin Street from the Grand Marais Realty Company.[1] Almost a year later on May 13, 1907, Mr. Johnson purchased two more lots, numbers 14 and 15 in block 20.[2] In November 9,1907, it was reported that Mr. Johnson was building a large, two-story barn on his lots. The barn was to be used as a feed stable in connection with the Grand Hotel across the street,[3] which John Johnson had been leasing since April 1906.[4]

In October 1908, the Grand Hotel, which John Johnson was leasing, burned to the ground. Whether or not the loss of the Grand Hotel prompted John Johnson to build his own saloon across the street, one can only speculate. However, it is a fact that in the fall of 1908 he did build a two-story structure on the northwest corner of First Avenue West and Wisconsin Street. This is the current location of Joynes Department Store. The local paper reported that "the lower floor was to be used as a saloon and the upper floors for living apartments."[5] Starting on December 3, 1908, the following advertisement was run in every issue of the local newspaper through April 1, 1909.

Advertisement in *Cook County News-Herald* on December 3, 1908.

Wisconsin Street Looking East. On left side of photo: Dr. Hick's Building, Grand Marais State Bank and John's New Place. Building behind John's New Place with roof showing is the old Court House building which was moved to this location in 1913.The bank building was built in the fall of 1916. *Circa 1917 (Photo courtesy of Cook County Historical Society.)*

Until 1914, the only other ad for John's New Place that appeared was a "For Rent Advertisement" in the local paper. The ad stated that his building was for rent and that it contained eight rooms on the second floor and could be used for a store, hotel or restaurant. A barn and root house in the rear of the building was also for rent.[6] No record has been found of anyone renting the buildings.

Following the death of John Johnson, in October 1922, a Probate Court Order distributed his estate on March 4, 1924. Erick and Karen Johnson (husband and wife) living in Sweden received one-third of the estate. Anna Christina N. Strandgren and Nils Strandgren (husband and wife), also living in Sweden, received one-third of the estate, and Jon [Joe] Johnson[ii] who was living in Duluth received one-third of the estate.[7] Jon and Erick were brothers of John and Anna was a sister. A few months later on December 8, 1924, the heirs in Sweden sold their interests in the properties to Jon Johnson.

Information about the use of the building prior to 1933 is very limited. The discovery of an old sign in the building does indicate that the second floor was used as a hotel or boarding house sometime during the years

Old Sign Found in Joynes' Storage Building, the former Johnson or Soderberg Building. *(Photo courtesy of Julie Joynes Carlson)*

[ii] In the newspaper account of John's death, the brother in Duluth is referred to as Joe. In the court order he is called Jon Johnson.

between 1909 and 1944. Sometime during this period the building was called the Bay View Hotel and sometimes the Shore View Hotel. On the second floor there were seven rooms and only one bathroom, which was typical for boarding houses and hotels in the early part of the last century.

The first floor was setup as a saloon and was used as such from 1909-1919. During the years of prohibition, 1920-1933, alcoholic beverages could not have been legally sold, but the first floor remained set up as a tavern.[8] Regarding this change in the business the article, which announced the death of John Johnson on October 27, 1922, stated that "In recent years he has conducted a soft drink and cigar store in his building on Wisconsin Street."[9]

Building Sold to Ruth Soderberg

On March 22, 1933, Jon Johnson, known locally as "Bear" Johnson, sold the building and the four lots, on which Joynes' store and storage building now sits, to Ruth Soderberg.[10] From that date on, the building became known as the Soderberg Building. Prior to purchasing Johnson's building, Ruth had owned and operated the Soderberg Dry Goods & Clothing Store in what today is the White Pine North building. She sold primarily women's clothes. She started her dry goods and clothing store on December 8,1923. Earlier Ruth had hired Andrew Shold to build a twenty-five foot square building as the first phase of her building. Later she hired Andrew Hedstrom to add another twenty-five feet to her building.[11]

In her new location Ruth opened the Grand Marais Ice Cream Store in July 1933. She used part of the second floor as her personal living quarters and rented out the other rooms. For the hotel part of the business I have been unable to determine which years Ruth called the hotel the Bay View, and which years the Shore View. Roger Nelson said it was called the Bay View in 1946, when his family operated a cafe on the lower level of the building.[12] But, when Milford Humphrey rented the first floor it was called the Shore View.

Earlier, in August 1932, Ruth began a "close out sale" of her inventory in her Dry Goods & Clothing Store.[13] This sale continued until late November 1933 when she ran an ad that stated that the balance of her stock would be moved to the Ice Cream Store where it would be for sale.[14] From her new store she sold what she called Grand Marais Ice Cream to restaurants, hotels, Civilian Conservation Corps camps, other stores, and to walk in customers.

There were several additional ads in the local newspaper for the Ice Cream Store in the fall of 1933, but in 1934 and 1935 the ads discontinued, except for an advertisement for ice cream and pies for Christmas in December 1934,[15] and for Easter in April 1935.[16] These advertisements appear to have been for orders in advance to take out.

The Photo Art Shop and Humphrey's Clothing

After Ruth moved her remaining inventory out of her Dry Goods & Clothing Store she rented the building to Milford and Ed Humphrey who were brothers. Ed had come to Cook County in the early 1930's, and in 1933 had set up a canteen near the CCC camp, which was located near McFarland Lake on the Arrowhead Trail. He sold candy, gum and photographic film and later shoes and suits to the boys.[17] He would send the film to be developed to Milford, who lived in Wheaton, Illinois, where he had started a photo service business after graduating from Wheaton College in 1932. Ed Humphrey soon began encouraging Milford to move to Grand Marais because he thought Milford could get a lot of business from the many CCC Camps in the county. Since business was not very profitable for Milford in his new venture in Wheaton during the depression, he moved to Grand Marais in July 1933, and started a photo finishing business. He first lived in Simon Backlund's house and set up a photo developing room in the basement. After the summer tourist season he set up a photo studio in a vacant dining room in Fred Sjoberg's Restaurant in September 1933.[18]

Advertisement in *Cook County News-Herald*, July 20, 1933, p. 3.

By the end of 1933, business was going well for Milford so he and Edward rented Ruth Soderberg's original building which was empty. Milford used the one side of the building for his Grand Marais Photo Service, and Ed started the Great Northern Dry Cleaning and Laundry Service in the other side. The two brothers lived in the back of the building sharing the area with two other men.[19] Approximately a year later Ed started selling men's clothes in his part of the store and by June 1935, was calling his business the Great Northern Men's Shop.[20]

Advertisement in *Cook County News-Herald*, September 7, 1933, p. 4.

By early 1936, the brothers decided to form a partnership and purchased the building from Ruth Soderberg on May 10, 1936, for $3,000.[21] The brothers not only purchased the building as partners, but apparently ran their businesses as a partnership. Milford soon began calling his part of the business the Photo Art Shop and Ed soon began to title his side of the store Humphrey's Clothing. During the World War II years of 1942-1945 Ed moved to Duluth and worked in the shipyards.

Milford continued to operate the business in Grand Marais, but was almost forced to close the store in 1944. He was in line to be drafted into the army, had passed his physical and was waiting to be called and had a "Closing Out Sale" in February 1944. Then suddenly the age limit was changed and he was found to be beyond the draft age. He revived the business with cash from his "Closing out Sale" and restocked the store with merchandise.[22] After the war Ed returned to Grand Marais and joined up again with Milford in the retail business.[23]

Due to the increase in their businesses they rented the first floor of the Shore View Hotel during the summer of 1952[24] as an expansion effort of the Photo Art Shop[25] and for storage.[26] The dating of this rental arrangement during the summer of 1952 indicates that the Humphrey brothers rented the store after it was moved to its current location by Howard Joynes. An aerial photo dated 1951, shows the building in its current location.

During this summer Russell Smith managed the store in the Soderberg building for Milford.[27] The rental of the Soderberg building by Humphrey brothers apparently was for only the one summer, but an article in the local

Advertisement in *Cook County News-Herald*, December 21, 1933, p. 3.

Advertisement in *Cook County News-Herald*, May 14, 1936, p. 4.

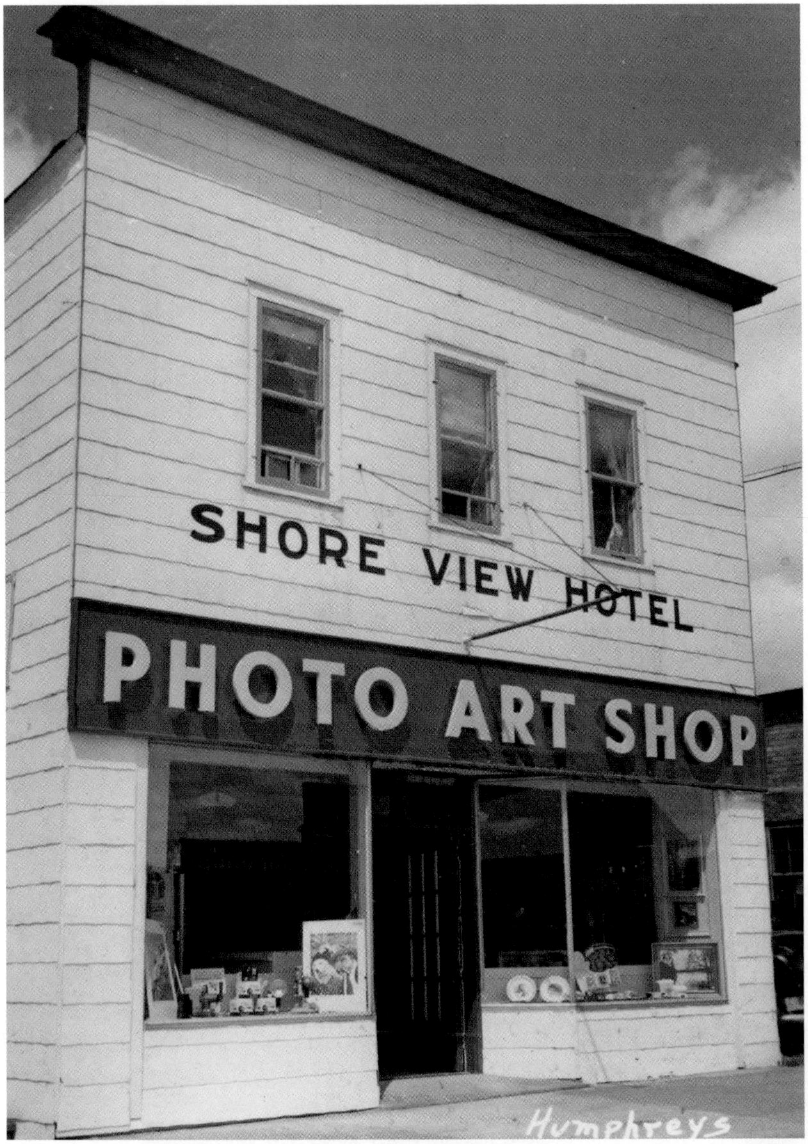

M. J. Humphrey's Photo Art Shop in the Shore View Hotel. Summer 1952.
(Photo courtesy of Cook County Historical Museum.)

newspaper in 1958 implies that they rented the building through the summer of 1956, operating the Photo Art Shop only during the summer months in the Shore View Hotel building.[28]

On September 1, 1955, the two brothers expanded their business by purchasing the lot where Fred Sjoberg's Cafe had once stood, and where Tony's Lunch was located. They built a new building on the lot and on August 5, 1957, Ed Humphrey opened Humphrey's Clothing Store in the new location.[29] This allowed the Photo Art Shop, which now included gifts and a florist shop, to have the entire building across the street.

Soon after opening the new store, the brothers began dissolving their partnership as a means of allowing for the smooth transition of their respective businesses to another generation. At this time Ed became the sole owner of Humphrey Clothing business, and Milford the sole owner of The Photo Art Shop business. In January 1964, the next step in dissolving the partnership took place when title to the clothing store land and building was transferred to Ed and presumable title to the Photo Art Store building and land to Milford.

The transition of ownership to the next generation for the clothing store took place on December 17, 1970, when Edward sold the

A postcard of Humphrey's New Clothing Store. *1957. (Postcard courtesy of Charles Humphrey.)*

Postcard of the Interior of the New Humphrey Store. *Circa 1957. (Postcard courtesy of Charles Humphrey.)*

Milford and Edward Humphrey at Grand Opening of their new store in 1957. *(Photo courtesy of Charles Humphrey.)*

business to his son Charles, via a corporation titled Humphreys Inc. Charles Humphrey had been working in the store since December 1963.[30] In about 1974, Charles and his wife Janie, purchased the building and land.[31] A few years later Janie started a Beauty Salon in the rear of the building. In 1995, Charles and Janie sold the building to Jan Sivertson.[32]

By 1973, Milford Humphrey was also making plans for retirement. His son Steve had been working with him for a few years, and the hope was that Steve would take over the ownership of the Photo Art Shop. Then tragedy struck when Steve died on June 15, 1973, from injuries in a motorcycle accident.[33]

During the next year Milford contacted Jim Larson about purchasing the business. Jim was a former resident of Grand Marais who had graduated from Bethel College and was working in the Twin Cities. After spending some time considering the opportunity to buy the business from Milford and moving back to Grand Marais, Jim and his wife, Jackie, purchased the Photo Art Shop business and building on July 1, 1974.[34] In 1998, they changed the name of their business to White Pine North.

Sivertson Gallery located in the building formerly housing Humphreys Clothing Store. The old Shore Theater building is on the right. *June 2008.*

White Pine North Gift Shop. *July 2008.*

The Soderberg Building

Ruth Soderberg, now in her new location in the old Shore View Hotel building continued to operate her ice cream store on the first floor. In addition to her home made ice cream she sold pies, pop, coffee and snack food, including her own home made potato chips.

During the forties Ruth developed severe arthritis and became bedridden.[35] On October 29, 1942, Ruth transferred the title of the property to her sister Edith Soderberg.[36] During this time Edith lived upstairs and cared for her sister. On September 9, 1944, Edith sold the property to Howard Joynes, for $5,000 with scheduled payments and with the stipulation that Edith would remove the old building as soon as Howard was ready to build on the lot. Because of circumstances related to WWII, Howard's plans to build a new store were delayed. As part of the sales agreement, Edith Soderberg, had full and complete use of the building and premises until Howard was ready to build.[37] Whether Edith kept the store open during the early or late forties is not certain.

It is known that Harry and Margaret Flaherty operated a cafe on the first floor of the building for about a year sometime between 1943 and the fall of 1945. Lil Anderson, who was a sister to Margaret remembers working in the cafe at the time for about a year.[38]

In the fall of 1945 through 1946, Edith rented the building to Mr. and Mrs. (Amy) Arvid Nelsen. They operated a cafe on the first floor and lived upstairs with their children. Amy's sister, Mrs. Mildred Backstrom, a widower, and her three children shared the upstairs with the Nelsen family.[39]

In December 1946 or early 1947, a Hall family rented the first floor and started a cafe called Hall's Eat Shop. They enlarged the dining area and served dinners and

A 1938 photo of a WPA crew putting in a cement sidewalk in front of the Soderberg Building. The building to the left is a barbershop and the Grand Marais State Bank is adjacent to the barber shop. *(Photo courtesy of the Cook County Historical Society.)*

short-order items. In April 1947, the local newspaper reported that "The Halls have built up quite a following for the brief time they have operated" the business.[40] I was not able to find out if the Halls lived upstairs when they operated the cafe. From the information available it appears that the Halls operated the Eat Shop for about a year. What the building was used for during the years of 1948 through 1951 is not clear.

On November 21, 1949, Howard and Rosemary Joynes received the deed for the land and building.[41]

OPEN

—FROM 5:30 a. m. to 12 o'clock Midnight—

SERVED REGULARLY:

DINNERS—and—SHORT ORDERS

A good place to meet your friends after the show.

Hall's Eat Shop

Advertisement in *Cook County News-Herald*, January 16, 1947, p. 8.

Aerial photo of Grand Marais. Note that the Soderberg Building has been moved to its new location. *1951. (Photo courtesy of Lois Pedersen Sundin.)*

Sometime prior to the fall of 1951, they had the building moved to its new location facing First Avenue West. Since then Joynes has used the building for storage space for their store. It remains as one of the oldest wood frame buildings in the business district. After the Soderberg building was moved Howard Joynes began building his new store on the corner, as was explained in the previous chapter.

(Endnotes)

1. Book O, Deed Record, p 2. Cook County Recorders Office, Grand Marais, MN.

2. Book Q, Deed Record, p 9. Cook County Recorders Office, Grand Marais, MN.

3. "TOPICS OF A WEEK," *Cook County Herald*, Nov. 9, 1907, p. 5.

4. TOPICS OF A WEEK," *Cook County Herald*, April 7, 1907, p. 3.

5. TOPICS OF A WEEK," *Cook County News-Herald*, November 5, 1908, p. 1.

6. "FOR RENT" Advertisement, *Cook County News-Herald*, June 18, 1914, p.1.

7. Book Q, Deed Record, p. 299. Cook County Recorders Office, Grand Marais, MN.

8. Interview with Bob Zimmerman, November 30, 2007.

9. "John Johnson of Grand Died Saturday Morning," *Cook County News-Herald*, October 26, 1922, p.1.

10. Book 8, Warranty Deed Record, p. 529, Cook County Recorders Office, Grand Marais, MN.

11. "The History of the Ruth Soderberg Building," Overlook, Cook County Historical Society, Summer 2008. p. 1.

12. Interview with Roger Nelson, April 3, 2008.

13. Close out sale advertisement, *Cook County News-Herald*, August 25, 1932, p. 4.

14. "The Balance of My Stock" Advertisement, *Cook County News-Herald*, November 23, 1933, p.4.

15. Advertisement, *Cook County News-Herald*, December 20, 1934, p. 2.

16. Advertisement, *Cook County News-Herald*, April 18, 1935, p. 4.

17. "Humphreys Observe 25th Year; Twice almost Gave Up Struggle," *Cook County News-Herald*, August 21, 1958.

18. "The History of the Photo Shop," *Cook County News-Herald*, November 17, 1983, p. 5.

19. "Humphreys Observe 25th Year; Twice almost Gave Up Struggle," *Cook County News-Herald*, August 21, 1958.

20. "Advertisement," *Cook County News-Herald*, June 27, 1935.

21. Book 11, Warranty Deed Record, pp. 225 & 226, Cook County Recorders Office, Grand Marais, MN.

22. "Humphreys Observe 25th Year; Twice almost Gave Up Struggle," *Cook County News-Herald*, August 21, 1958.

23. Kathy Humphrey Stoltz, "Edward Humphrey," *The Humphrey Saga*, Edited by Milford Humphrey, 1993, p.37. (Mimeographed.)

24. "Humphreys Observe 25th Year; Twice almost Gave Up Struggle," *Cook County News-Herald*, August 21, 1958.

25. "Humphreys Been 'at it' 35 Years," *Cook County News-Herald*, November 28, 1968. p. 1.

26. Interview with Charles Humphrey, August 13, 2008.

27. Interview with Charles Humphrey, August 13, 2008.

28. "Humphreys Observe 25th Year; Twice almost Gave Up Struggle," *Cook County News-Herald*, August 21, 1958.

29. "Humphreys Have Open House Friday," *Cook County News-Herald*, August 15, 1957, p. 1.

30. Interview with Charles Humphrey, August 25, 2008.

31. Kathy Humphrey Stoltz, "Edward Humphrey," *The Humphrey Saga*, Edited by Milford Humphrey, 1993, p.37. (Mimeographed.)

32. Interview with Charles Humphrey, August 13, 2008.

33. Ruth Humphrey, "Ruth's Writing," an unpublished booklet entitled, *The Humphrey Saga,* Edited by Milford Humphrey, 1993, pp. 28-29.

34. "Photo Art Shop Ownership Will Change on July 1," *Cook County News-Herald*, June 6, 1974, p. 1.

35. Interview with Hazel McClanahan, a niece of Ruth Soderberg, July 12, 2007.

36. Book 10, Warranty Deed Record, p. 581, Cook County Recorders Office, Grand Marais, MN.

37. Warrant Deed, Filed December 30, 1944, Cook County Recorders Office, Grand Marais, MN.

38. Interview with Lillian Anderson, July 1, 2008.

39. Interview with Roger Nelson, April 3, 2008.

40. "Cafe 'Doll Up' For Summer Guests," *Cook County News-Herald*, April 24, 1947, p.1.

41. Book 13, Deed Record, Cook County Recorders Office, Grand Marais, MN.

Chapter 7

Other Hotels and Boarding Houses

Introduction

This chapter includes a brief history of hotels and boarding houses located in the central area of Grand Marais that were not mentioned in the previous chapters. Lodging facilities outside the central area of town are not included in this list because they are outside the basic focus of this book.

Amyotte Place

Another hotel or boarding house built during the early 1900's was a two-story frame building owned by Fred Amyotte. He began building the 20 x 30 foot building in December of 1904.[1] By the end of the next month the local paper carried an advertisement for rooms and a restaurant and lunchroom at the back of Amyotte's Place.

The place seems to have been more of a boarding house than a hotel. The location of Amyotte's Place is not clear from the information available; however, we do know that Fred Amyotte sold lot 5 in block 31, January 18, 1906. This lot was just north of the Sterling Hotel and is now the northern portion of East Bay

Advertisement in *Cook County Herald*, on January 28, 1905. This ad ran weekly, at least through July 1, 1905.

Suites Property. It seems reasonable to speculate that this was the location of his boarding house.

Hussey's Boarding House

In 1907, John and Anna Hussey built a house on the southwest corner of Highway 61 and First Avenue West, which currently is the location of the American Legion Post's parking lot. The Husseys had six children: Thomas, F. Castle "Cac," Michael, Leo, Vivian and Nellie. The 1920 census listed Mr. and Mrs. Hussey and their children, F. Castle "Cac," Tom, and Nellie and a boarder as living in the house. Over the years the home became more of a boarding house. John Hussey died in 1931 and Anna Hussey died in 1957. In Mrs. Hussey's obituary in the local paper it was reported that she owned probably the largest residence in the village and had rented rooms to tourists in the summer months.[2] During the 1930's and 1940's, many teachers in the local school boarded

The Hussey Boarding House is in the middle of the picture, below the Arrowhead Hotel. Midway Garage is on the right. *1951, (The picture is a portion of an aerial photo courtesy of Lois Pedersen Sundin.)*

The Hussey House. *Circa 1920. (Photo courtesy of Cook County Historical Museum.)*

with Mrs. Hussey. Tom Hussey, worked in the Recorders Office in the Court House, never married and lived in the building until shortly before it was sold in 1967.[3]

The Hussey House Being Moved. November 1967. *(Photo courtesy of Cook County Historical Society.)*

On the left end of the house in this picture it appears that an addition had been added to the building sometime after 1951. The above picture shows four windows on the second floor and the other pictures show only three.

In 1967, Harold and Sherman Benson, who owned the Midway Garage, bought the lot and the Hussey house from Ellen Hussey and the estate of Tom Hussey. The Bensons wanted the lot for a parking lot. In September, they contacted Marty Clark, who owned the Gunflint Construction Company, and offered the house to him if he would move it off the lot by January 1, 1968. Marty agreed, and moved the house to a lot he owned on the northeast corner of 11th Street and 1st Avenue West. Marty hired Tim Mathisen to move the building and they succeeded in moving the house and setting it on a foundation by the deadline.[4] Shortly after moving the building, Marty moved to Ohio for about a year. During this brief time period, Marty's parents, Mr. and Mrs. David Clark sold the Gunflint Motel, which they owned, and as part of some family business, Marty gave them title to the lot and house.

When Marty came back to Grand Marais in 1970, he and his dad, with the help of Donnie Lehto, Butch Nelson, and Lonny and Dwight Smith removed the inside walls of the second floor and built a new roof over the first floor inside the existing second floor and roof.[5] After the new roof was in place they removed the original second floor walls and roof.[6] This somewhat unusual procedure made it possible to replace the roof without the risk of rain leaking into the first floor of the house. Thus the former Hussey boarding house became the home of Mr. and Mrs. David Clark. It stands on the same corner today, but one would never recognize it as the former Hussey House.

The Arrowhead Hotel

The next major hotel built in Grand Marais after the Broadway, Grand and Paine hotels was the Arrowhead Hotel. It was located on the northwest corner of 1st Avenue West and

Postcard of Arrowhead Hotel. *Circa 1930. (Courtesy of Cook County Historical Museum.)*

Arrowhead Hotel with first floor corner used as a Rexall Drug Store. *Circa 1955. (Photo courtesy of Cook County Historical Museum.)*

Highway 61. Ed Nunstedt began constructing the hotel on April 1, 1925. In June 1925, the local paper reported that "...the new hotel is fast shaping into a modern hostelry. It will have 36 rooms available for the traveling public, with a number of private baths and hot and cold running water in every room."[7] Ed Nunstedt operated the hotel for about ten years.

After Mr. Nunstedt, the hotel was operated by Art Fawcett and later by other owners for short periods of time. When the hotel was closed in 1969, it was managed by Frank Kimball and owned by Clark and John McElevey. After the hotel closed the top two floors were removed and the remainder of the building continued to be used for the Peterson Drug Store, Chuck's Barber Shop and Bernice's Beauty Shop.[8]

The Shoreline Motel

A new era in motel building in Grand Marais began in September 1952, when excavation began on what was to become the Shoreline Motel. The motel was and is still located next to the Cook County Museum on Broadway and on the East Harbor. The hotel was to have 30 rooms, all with private baths. The materials used in the construction of this building represented the first shift from the sole use of wood in the construction of hotel and motel buildings in Grand Marais.

Entrance to Shoreline Motel. *Circa 1955. (Photo courtesy of County Historical Museum.)*

Postcard photo of lakeside of Shoreline Motel. *Circa 1955. (Postcard courtesy of Bill and Beth Blank.)*

The headline for the article announcing the beginning of construction was entitled, "New Fireproof Hotel in Village Started Here," The article went on to explain that:

> The main construction will be of steel framework with slag aggregate blocks, which are considered stronger than cinder block. The subfloor will be of Perlite aggregate, which is not quite as hard as cement, with possibly tile covering. The roof will be steel with a build-up [sic] surfacing.[9]

When the construction of the hotel was announced, Bernard Skoog and Glenn Joynes were listed as the owners. Glenn was a brother of Howard Joynes who was mentioned earlier in this book as the owner of Joynes Department Store.

When the Hotel opened for business in August of 1954, Henry Ulhorn had joined the ownership group.[10] Three years later in late November or early December 1957,[11] George Peet acquired a majority ownership in the motel by purchasing Ulhorn's and Skoog's interest in the property. He assumed management of the motel in early December and re-opened the dining room just before Christmas.

Sometime during the next year or two George Peet acquired total ownership of the hotel property, which included a house across Broadway, by purchasing Glenn

Postcard photo of dining room of Shoreline Motel. *Circa 1955. (Postcard courtesy of Bill and Beth Blank.)*

The Shoreline Motel. September *2008.*

Joynes' interest in the motel. Part of Glenn Joynes' investment in the property was his ownership of the land on which the motel was built.[12] In recent years George Peet and his son Barney have been responsible for the management of the Shoreline Motel, the Super 8 Motel and Aspen Lodge in Grand Marais. The Peet family owns the three motels. Mark Sandbo has been their onsite General Manager for a few years.

The Harbor Inn

In September 1961, Carl and Grace Nunstedt purchased the lots on which the Harbor Inn is located today from B. Van Johnson[13] and the Ogema Land & Abstract Co.[14] This was part of the same parcel of land on which Mrs. J. Spooner and Mr. and Mrs. Fred Andert laid the foundation for an 80 room hotel in 1922.[i] As was pointed out in Chapter 3, that hotel was never built and parts of the foundation were still visible when the Nunstedts purchased the lot. However a motel was soon to be built on the site.

Postcard of the Hub Restaurant before motel was built. The building on the left is the Ogema Real Estate Office. *Circa 1962. (Photo by M. J. Humphrey, Postcard courtesy of Jim and Jane Shinners.)*

In 1961-1962, the Nunstedts built and opened the drive-in restaurant called the Hub as the first phase of their new business. The Hub had a small indoor seating area in addition to the outdoor drive-up option and an apartment upstairs where Mr. and Mrs.

---

[i]In 1938, Mr. and Mrs. F. A. Andert and Jessie Spooner had sold lots 12 through 15 of this parcel to Ed Nunstedt [Book 13, Warranty Deed Record, p. 4, Cook County Recorders Office, Grand Marais, MN.] and lot 16 to Homer and Pearl Underwood in September 1944. [Book 12, Warranty Deed Record, p. 567, Cook County Recorders Office, Grand Marais, MN.]

In October 1944, Ed Nunstedt sold lots 12 through 15 to Mr. and Mrs. Underwood. [Book 12, Warranty Deed Record, p.612, Cook County Recorders Office, Grand Marais, MN.]

In November 1947 The Underwoods sold lots 15 & 16 to the Grand Marais American Legion Post # 413 [Book 16, Warranty Deed Record, p. 9, Cook County Recorders Office, Grand Marais, MN.] who sold the lots to A. V. Johnson in October 1949. This process gave A. V. Johnson ownership of lots 12 through 16. In 1953, Mr. and Mrs. A. V. Johnson transferred the title to the property to his son, B. Van Johnson and his wife, Josephine. [Book 13, Deed Record, p. 486, Cook County Recorders Office, Grand Marais, MN.] Through a couple of more transactions Ogema Land & Abstract Company ended up with the south 48 feet of lot 16 in 1955, and Carl and Grace Nunstedt with the northern part of the lot in 1961.

A postcard photo of the Hub Motel and Restaurant. The back of the card included the following information: “Rooms have tub and shower, vanity, hot water heat, free T.V....Carl and Grace Nunstedt owners.” *Circa 1966. (Postcard courtesy of Jim and Jane Shinners.)*

Postcard of Harbor Inn Motel and Restaurant. *Circa 1974. (Post card courtesy of Bill and Beth Blank.)*

Harbor Inn Motel and the Wild Onion Restaurant. *June 2008*

Carl Nunstedt and their family lived. Carl Nunstedt was acquainted with the restaurant and hotel business due to the fact that his father, Ed Nunstedt, had built and owned the Arrowhead Hotel.

In 1965, Carl and Grace built and opened the motel phase of the business. They ran the restaurant and motel until 1973, when they sold it to the Grand Marais Hotel Company, Inc., which George and Marge Peet owned.[15]

When the Peets took over the business they converted the existing kitchen area to more dining space, added a larger kitchen area in the back of the building, and remodeled the motel.[16] The remodeling included adding insulation and paneling to the exterior walls and painting the building green. They also changed the name of the business to the Harbor Inn and Restaurant. In 1979, the Peets sold the business to Ted and Carol Backlund.[17] An interesting aspect of this sale was the fact that Carol was a daughter of Mr. and Mrs. Carl Nunstedt, the original owners and builders of the motel and restaurant.

On February 28, 1997, Ted and Carol Backlund sold the business to Jim and Jane Shinners.[18] In 2001, the Shinners began remodeling the exterior of the building by adding a new roof. During the next two years they added new trim and awnings, and painted the building with a new color scheme.[19] This latest new look is shown in the above photo.

In 2007, the Shinners began to cut back on their work schedule by leasing the restaurant to Chris and Brigette Nies. The Nies's renamed the restaurant the Wild Onion Cafe. For most of the years that the restaurant has been open the various owners have closed the restaurant from about mid-October to mid-April. The Shinners continue to manage the motel which is open all year.

(Endnotes)

1. "TOPICS OF A WEEK," *Cook County Herald*, December 24, 1904, p. 5.

2. "Anna Hussey, Who Came Here as Col. Colvill Housekeeper, Dies at 92," *Cook County News-Herald*, January 17, 1957 p. 1

3. Interview with Eleanor Waha, June 25, 2008.

4. "Picture and article about moving Hussey house," *Cook County News-Herald*, November 30, 1967, p. 1.

5. Interview with Marty Clark, August 9, 2008.

6. Interview with Donald Lehto, June 12, 2008.

7. "News-ettes of Grand Marais and Vicinity," *Cook County News-Herald*, June 4, 1925, p. 4.

8. "Arrowhead Hotel Has Been Closed," *Cook County News-Herald*, January 23, 1969, p. 1.

9. "New Fireproof Hotel in Village Started Here," *Cook County News-Herald*, September 25, 1952, p. 1.

10. "Shoreline Hotel Opens, *Cook County News-Herald*, August 5, 1954, p. 1.

11. "Shoreline Hotel Gets New Manager; George Peet Now in Charge," *Cook County News-Herald*, December 5, 1957 p. 1.

12. Telephone conversation with George Peet, June 28, 2008.

13. Book 23, Deed Record, p.515, Cook County Recorders Office, Grand Marais, MN.

14. Book 24, Deed Record, p. 481, Cook County Recorders Office, Grand Marais, MN.

15. Book 95, Deed Record, p. 475, Cook County Recorders Office, Grand Marais, MN.

16. Telephone conversation with George Peet, June 28, 2008.

17. Book 108, Deed Record, p. 255, Cook County Recorders Office, Grand Marais, MN.

18. Book 162, Deed Record, p. 640, Cook County Recorders Office, Grand Marais, MN.

19. Interview with Jane Shinner, July 1, 2008. *Cook County News-Herald*

Chapter 8

Other Property Near the Blue Water Cafe

The Standard and Shell Stations

On the southwest corner of 1st Street and Wisconsin Avenue, and across the street from the Blue Water Cafe, a Standard Oil gas station was located for many years. The ownership of the corner by Standard Oil Company of Indiana began on August 8, 1924, when it purchased a lot 100 feet wide fronting on Wisconsin Street and west of Madison Street, which is now First Avenue West, for $3,000 from the Grand Marais Realty Company.[1] On January 8, 1926, The Standard Oil Company purchased an additional seventy-five feet of land adjacent to and west of the original parcel. This parcel was purchased from Mr. and Mrs. (Aleda) J. T. Joynes for $1,200.[2] The Joynes had purchased the parcel from Mr. and Mrs. (Irene) Morris H. Olson on July 27, 1925, for $1000.[3] The Olsons had purchased the parcel from E. E. Johnson on November 13, 1924.[4] Morris Olson also purchased the property being developed as Cascade Lodge in 1926, and became one of three shareholders in Cascade Lodge, Inc. in 1927.[5]

Edward Ellsworth "E. E." Johnson, was not a relative of Charlie or A. Van Johnson. E. E. Johnson was born in Wisconsin, and

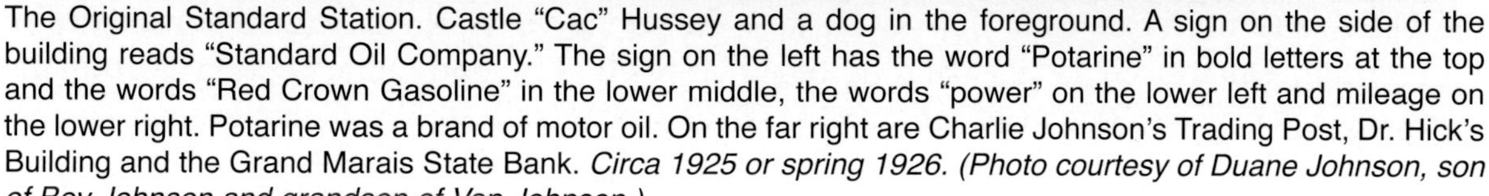

The Original Standard Station. Castle "Cac" Hussey and a dog in the foreground. A sign on the side of the building reads "Standard Oil Company." The sign on the left has the word "Potarine" in bold letters at the top and the words "Red Crown Gasoline" in the lower middle, the words "power" on the lower left and mileage on the lower right. Potarine was a brand of motor oil. On the far right are Charlie Johnson's Trading Post, Dr. Hick's Building and the Grand Marais State Bank. *Circa 1925 or spring 1926. (Photo courtesy of Duane Johnson, son of Bev Johnson and grandson of Van Johnson.)*

Standard Oil Company Station. Note Johnson's New Place (Shore View Hotel) across Wisconsin Street from station and Arrowhead Hotel in background. Note walk way from shore to concrete pillars where ships anchored.

received his early education in Wisconsin public schools and later a law degree from the University of Wisconsin. He moved to Port Arthur, Ontario, in 1919, when he became manager of the Pigeon River Lumber Company. This was the beginning of a successful career in lumber and shipping.[6] As part of his expanding business interests he purchased all the unplatted portion of Lot 1, Section 21, and Lot 5, Section 21 from the Grand Marais Realty Company, on August 15, 1924.[7] E. E. Johnson also purchased part

The building on the right is the Tourist Hotel. This picture was taken sometime between 1926 and fall of 1931. *(Photo is a portion of a post card courtesy of Bill and Beth Blank.)*

of Lot 4, Section 21 about this time. The land in Lot 1 and Lot 5 included the seventy-five foot wide parcel referred to above which he sold to Morris Olson and the land along the harbor that eventually became Bear Tree Park.

The original phase of the Standard Oil operation on the harbor is pictured on the first page of this chapter. Soon thereafter, the site was developed to include a bulk oil and gasoline storage distribution site. I was not able to determine the exact year or years that the

Standard Station with storage tanks. The building to the right of the tanks is for storage of oil and gas barrels and supplies.

bulk oil facilities were built, but it is clear from photos that it was completed by the fall of 1931. It is possible that the bulk facility was built in stages. The facilities included big cement pillars and a catwalk between shore and a pillar out in the bay. This made it possible for ships to anchor behind the station and unload their load of fuel by pumping it into storage tanks on shore.

A. W. Miller was in charge of the original station until September of 1925, when F.

The Shore Theater is on the right near the shore. *Circa 1938. (Photo a portion of a postcard courtesy of Bill and Beth Blank.)*

Castle "Cac" Hussey[8] and Einer Allen took over the operation.[9] "Cac" Hussey continued to manage the station until June 1936, when he was hired to manage the new Shell Station, located at the intersection of Wisconsin Street and Highway 61, where the Java Moose Coffee Shop is currently located. Val Dalbec and Homer Underwood had purchased the land for the new station from F. A. Andert, one of the former owners of the Tourist Hotel, and had begun building the gas station in March 1935.[10]

Entire post card photo of Grand Marais Harbor with rafts of logs. *Circa 1938. (Postcard courtesy of Bill and Beth Blank.)*

According to a June 1936 newspaper article, the Shell Petroleum Company had purchased the station from the Dalbecs

Original Standard Station. *Circa 1936. (Photo Courtesy of Mike Quaife.)*

and Underwoods, but Val Dalbec's daughter, Lois told me that they never sold the station to Shell Petroleum Company.[11] What happened is that Val Dalbec and Homer Underwood made arrangements with the Shell Petroleum Company to sell Shell products at the new station. Then they hired "Cac" Hussey to manage the station. Val Dalbec was the wholesale agent, commonly called the bulk agent, for the Standard Oil Company, at the time. This was a position he held from the early 1930's until about 1954. He was also Mayor of Grand Marais for seventeen years, being first elected in 1938.[12]

Original Standard Station with Bulk Tanks on the right. *1936. (Photo courtesy of Mike Quaife.)*

Outdoor hoist at Original Standard Station. *Circa 1936. (Photo courtesy of Mike Quaife.)*

Being the bulk agent for the Standard Oil Company involved selling and hauling the gas and fuel oil from the storage tanks on the harbor to several retail Standard Stations in the county and to individual homes and businesses with smaller fuel storage tanks. The bulk business also included gas and fuel oil being delivered by ship in barrels. Eventually the bulk business involved two to three drivers and trucks.

Following Hussey's management of the Shell Station Fritz Lindquist leased the property and managed the business from about 1945 to 1956. Peter Floe managed the station from 1956 until 1971 when he retired and the Shell Station was discontinued.[13] Val Dalbec never managed the retail Standard Service Station. It was a separate business entity from the bulk business. When the separation of the operations took place is unclear. Perhaps this happened when Dalbec was hired by Standard Oil of Indiana in the early 1930's.

After "Cac" Hussey resigned from his position at the Standard Station, Morris D. Quaife leased the station from the Standard Oil Company of Indiana. Morris operated the business under the title Quaife's Standard Service until September 1958.[14]

In March 1950, the Standard Oil Company announced their plans to build a new station

The Shell Station at the intersection of Highway 61 and Wisconsin Street. *Circa 1936. (Photo courtesy of Carol J. Henry, daughter of Mr. & Mrs. Homer Underwood.)*

on the lot. The new building was completed during that year and the original station building was moved over to a lot on Highway 61, behind what today is the Harbor Inn Motel. There it served as a tourist Information building for several years.

The next lessee was Jerry Malner, who operated the business as Malner's Standard Service until 1962.[15] Joe Jurek was the next operator of the station. He leased the business from 1962 until September 26, 1966, when Gene Erickson took over the operation. In 1970, the Standard Oil Company again rebuilt the station. Prior to rebuilding the station the bulk tanks were moved to a location approximately two blocks south of what is now the Sawtooth Lumber Company.

In 1977, Gene purchased the business, building, and land from the Standard Oil Company. Gene's last day of selling gas was December 22, 1998, but he kept the repair and towing part of the business open until June 22, 2000. The City of Grand Marais had signed a purchase agreement with Gene and Barbara in 1998 for the land and the building.

The new Standard Station, which was built in 1950. There were two bays for servicing cars to the right of the photo. *(Photo courtesy of Mike Quaife.)*

Gene's decision to quit selling gas was partially based on a new state government requirement that gas station operators had to show proof, by October 15, 1998, that they were in the process of replacing underground tanks and pipes. This new environmental regulation

The Shell Station, with the Hub Motel and Restaurant in the background on the right and the Tourist Information Center on the left. *Circa 1964. (Photo courtesy of Lois Pedersen Sundin.)*

The Shore Theater, El Ray Cafe and Standard Station after November 1960 storm. *(Photo courtesy of Ethel Leng.)*

The Standard Station. *1997. (Photo courtesy Gene Erickson.)*

was the result of underground leakage problems in many areas. The cost of such a requirement and other remodeling costs caused many owners of older stations to sell their businesses. Thus, Gene and Barbara Erickson began the process of selling their property on the harbor. After many months of negotiations, on February 22, 2000, they sold the building and land to the Minnesota Trust for Public Land, who immediately sold the property to the City of Grand Marais.[16] By involving the Trust in this sale, the Ericksons and the city were able to create a transaction that benefited both parties.

Bear Tree Park

On May 25, 1945, the Grand Marais Village Council purchased the strip of property, west of the Standard Oil Station to where Highway 61 and Wisconsin Street meet today. This property was to become Bear Tree Park. The village purchased the parcel from Leslie H. Johnson for $1,000.[17] Leslie H. Johnson, was a son of A. Van Johnson and nephew of Charlie Johnson. Leslie Johnson had purchased the parcel on May 15, 1940, from Mr. and Mrs. L. P. Hirmer,[18] who had purchased the parcel on May 29, 1939, from the Whitney Corporation.[19] On February 9, 1926, The Whitney Corporation had purchased the land from Morris Olson,[20] who had purchased the land as part of a larger parcel from E. E. Johnson on November 13, 1924.[21] E. E. Johnson had purchased the land from the Grand Marais Realty Company on August 15, 1924.[22]

Postcard photo of Bear Tree Park. *Circa 1950's. (Postcard courtesy of Bill and Beth Blank.)*

The above series of transactions involving the Bear Tree Park parcel and the Standard Oil Station site are excellent examples of land around the harbor frequently changing ownership. Some of these changes undoubtedly were for investment purposes with the hope that the land would quickly increase in value. Some transactions may have been part of land trades or payment for other business transactions. It is fair to speculate regarding such factors because it was not unusual to have the payment for a parcel recorded for "one dollar and other good and valuable considerations." For some situations, such as the purchase by the Whitney Corporation and Standard Oil Company, the intent was to actually use the land.

The Whitney Corporation, (which in some legal documents was called the Whitney Brothers Company, and sometimes Whitney Material Company) was a Wisconsin corporation with Duluth as its place of business. During the 1920's, and perhaps earlier, the company purchased several parcels of land on the Grand Marais Harbor and on the East Bay, which included the gravel under the water bordering the parcels. It appears that selling and hauling gravel from the east and west bays of Grand Marais for use in Duluth was the primary interest of the Whitney Corporation in Grand Marais. When Harbor Park was created, Bear Tree Park became part of the larger park parcel.

The bottom part of the plaque reads as follows: "Dedicated to the town of Grand Marais in grateful appreciation of generous and continuing cooperation extended to the Minneapolis School of Art in the development of the Town Hall Art Colony." Erected and Dedicated in 1953. Sculpture Raymond J. Cormley.

The plaque at the site of the sculpture.

Lake Superior Trading Post

The land south of the Blue Water Cafe on the east side of 1st Street remained vacant until the early 1940's. Ray and Mabel Sjoberg on August 8, 1940, sold the land on which the current Lake Superior Trading Post is located to Sidney and Cyril Kluck, who used it as a base for their fishing business. During the 1940's, Sidney's brother Ed also fished with him. In 1948, Sidney moved to California, where he died in 1954.[23]

On July 7, 1964, Cyril, a nephew of Sidney, became the sole owner of the parcel when the heirs of Sidney transferred their portion of the property to him. On the same day, Cyril Kluck sold the property to Edward

Bear Tree Park Summer 2007

(Eddie) and Lillian Anderson. The Klucks had built a small building for their fishing business on the property, which Eddie started using in 1956. It is most likely that Eddie built the smoke house on the property in the late 1950's, which was part of his popular business.

Eddie Anderson was a commercial fisherman, during the 1940's and 1950's, who operated out of the old dock building which was located on the east side of the harbor by the lake when Eddie took over the business. The U. S. Forest Service or the Coast Guard owned the dock at the time and Eddie paid a fee of about $25 per month for renting the dock and building.[24] In late March of 1956, the building was completely destroyed by fire. Following the fire Eddie was able to operate his business from Kluck's property.[25] How long Cyril Kluck continued to fish from the site is unclear. The facts indicate that Eddie continued to use, and presumably rented, the property from Cyril until he and

Downtown Grand Marais. Note: Soderberg Building has been moved. Du Nord Cafe has not been built and Kluck's Fish House is in the foreground. *Circa1951. (Photo Courtesy of Lois Pedersen Sundin.)*

the current Coast Guard Station. In the early 1940's, Eddie bought all Jens Erickson's boats, nets and other fishing equipment and took over his rental arrangement for the building on the dock. At the time Jens was retiring and some of his nets were out in Lillian purchased the site in 1964.

Eddie and Lillian Anderson sold the land in 1971 to Ed and John Viren. As part of the sale Eddie and Lillian retained the right to use the smokehouse and retail fish house,

Eddie Anderson's Fish House and Coast Guard Station. *Circa Early 1950's. (Photo by Milford Humphrey.)*

which was located on the lakeside of the Trading Post after it was built. Eddie continued his fish business on the Trading Post property until his death in 1984. Following Eddie's death Lillian sold the business to Bob Howard who had worked with Eddie a couple summers. Bob operated the business through the 1986 summer and fall tourist season and then sold it to Brad and Karen Ranning.

Soon after purchasing the property Ed and John Viren began constructing what would become the Lake Superior Trading Post on the harbor. Prior to February 1971, Ed had been the pastor of Mount Rose Chapel in Grand Portage for seventeen years, and John had a veterinarian practice in White Bear Lake, Minnesota. The building had two stories and covered an area 55 x 60 feet with an open ceiling area inside. One-third of the lower level was used for John's veterinarian practice and the remainder of the building was for retail purposes.[26]

Eddie's Fish Business Building on the left and his smoke house on the right. *1960. (Photo courtesy of Nita Anderson, Eddie's daughter.)*

Eddie Anderson Smoking Fish. *Circa 1960. (Photo courtesy of Nita Anderson.)*

The June 24, 1971, issue of the local paper announced that the Lake Superior Trading Post was now open. The article continued as follows:

> Finishing touches on the Trading Post are being completed as the stock is filled out by the owners, Ed and Donna Viren and John and Janice Viren of Grand Portage.
>
> The shop features Indian handmade crafts, flown in from Ontario, north of the Albany River, where there are no roads; and from the Canadian Arctic, where crafts are made by the Eskimo and the Northern Cree Indians.
>
> Dean and Bobbi Jernigan will be leather workers. Besides handmade leather crafts, the Trading Post will have a good selection of moccasins and boots.
>
> In the gift line, the Virens will handle Scandinavian imports, wood items, soaps, candles, jewelry, and souvenirs....
>
> The store also features a complete sporting goods department, staffed by William "Bucko" Bushman. Tom Durham will be the shop mechanic and will handle out-board motor sales and repairs. Rick Ossanna will be the Flying Service pilot and also help in the store.
>
> The Trading Post portion of the store will feature furs of all kinds, maple syrup, maple sugar, and maple sugar

Eddie Anderson Smoking Fish. *Circa 1970. ((Photo courtesy of Nita Anderson.)*

candy, wild rice, teas, and other trading post items.[27]

Shortly after the Trading Post was opened Stan Fredrickson of Minneapolis purchased a 10 percent interest in the operation. Then in 1973, Richard Humphrey and Philip Peterson purchased controlling interest in the Trading Post. Richard Humphrey became the full time manager of the business and Philip was involved in the capacity of advisory manager, concentrating primarily on buying and promotional activities. The Viren brothers remained as participating stockholders.

A short time after the sale, Dr. John Viren and a partner opened a Kentucky Fried Chicken franchise in a building at the intersection of Broadway and Highway 61, which George Peet owned. The South of the Border Cafe is currently located in the building. John Viren also moved his veterinary practice to the lower level of the building.

Ed Viren stayed on in the trading post business concentrating primarily on the outfitting end of the business.[28] About a year and a half later Phillip Peterson sold his interests in the business to Richard Humphrey, who was president of the corporation. The Virens and Stan Fredrickson remained as stockholders.[29] Eventually the Virens and Stan Fredrickson sold their interest in the corporation to the Humphreys.

In the late 1970's, the Humphreys tore down the original fish house and built a new building to house both Eddie's Fish House and a deli on the lakeside. The deli was a summer operation in which they sold items such as ice cream, sandwiches, pop and coffee.

Richard Humphrey was very active in a wide range of community organizations and was mayor of Grand Marais from 1974 to 1981. In February 1982, Richard Humphrey and his son, Eric were skiing in Banff, Alberta, Canada, when he was stricken with a cerebral aneurism. After two surgeries in Calgary, Alberta Richard passed away on March 15,

The Original Trading Post Building was built adjacent to Eddie Anderson's Fish House. Note that the front of the Fish House was located closer to the street than the entrance of the Trading Post. *Circa 1975. (Photo courtesy of Russell and Linda Zenk.)*

Lake Superior Trading Post after Eddie Anderson's Fish House was torn down and replaced with a new building housing the Fish House and a Deli. Photo late 1970's. *(Photo courtesy Russell and Linda Zenk.)*`

at 43 years of age. His illness and death were the result of congenital complication and not due to skiing or other activities.[30]

After Richard's death, his wife Linda took over the management of the trading post. As part of the process of adjusting to her new role as manager of the trading post Linda closed the deli operation for the summer of 1982. A few months later on February 3, 1983, Bonnie Swanson opened Pierre's Pizza in the space formerly occupied by the deli.[31] On December 1, 1986, Bonnie sold the business to Roy and Judy Steinbrecker, who operated the pizza business in the same location for just over a year. In 1987, the Steinbreckers relocated Pierre's Pizza to the building west of the current Holiday Gas Station on Highway 61.[32]

Linda Humphrey married Russell Zenk, an architect in 1984. By 1987, they had made plans to expand the store and construction of a new addition was almost completed in May of 1988, when tragedy struck. On May 8, an arsonist set fire to

The New Fish House and Deli Building after the Deli was changed to Pierre's Pizza. *Circa 1983. (Photo courtesy of Russell and Linda Zenk.)*

the building and it was completely destroyed, including Eddie Anderson's Fish House, which had just opened two days earlier with Brad and Karen Ranning as the new owners. Russell Zenk had planned to relocate his architectural businesses into the new addition at the end of May, but was spared the loss of his business by not having moved in earlier.[33]

Eddies Fish House on the left and Pierre's Pizza on the right. *Circa 1985. (Photo courtesy of Bernice Howard.)*

This was a terrible loss to the Zenks and the community. Especially, after the Benson's Midway Building on the corner of First Avenue West and Highway 61 had burned to the ground earlier in January 1988.[34] This left two major businesses and lots in the town depressingly empty during the summer of 1988.

Pierre's Pizza. *Circa 1985. (Photo courtesy of Bernice Howard.)*

Lake Superior Trading Post. *July 2007.*

The good news for the community was that both owners decided to promptly rebuild. Russell Zenk soon began designing a new building and construction of the new Trading Post began in December.[35] The new Lake Superior Trading Post was open in May 1989 in time for the summer tourist season. The new Midway Building opened early in the summer of the same year.

(Endnotes)

1. Book 5, Warranty Deed Record, p. 593, Recorders Office, Cook County Court House, Grand Marais, MN

2. Book 6, Warranty Deed Record, p. 103, Recorded January 14, 1926, Recorders Office, Cook County Court House, Grand Marais, MN.

3. Book 4, Deed Record, P. 452, Recorded October 15, 1925, Recorders Office, Cook County Court House, Grand Marais, MN.

4. Book 2, Quit Claim Deed Record, P. 149, Recorded November 14, 1925, Recorders Office, Cook County Court House, Grand Marais, MN.

5. Eugene Glader, Cascade Lodge, Cascade Lodge, 3719 W. Highway 61, Lutsen, MN, 2005, pp. 21-27.

6. J. P. Bertrand, Timber Wolves, Thunder Bay Historical Society, Thunder Bay, Ontario, 1997, pp. 15 & 143.

7. Book 1, Quit Claim Deed Record, p. 267, Recorded August 16, 1924, Recorders Office, Cook County Court House, Grand Marais, MN.

8. "AMY BACKLUND AND C. HUSSEY MARRIED SAT.," *Cook County News-Herald*, October 15,1931, p.1.

9. "News-ettes of Grand Marais and Vicinity," *Cook County News-Herald*, September 10,1925, p.4.

10. "New Filling Sta. Building Started," *Cook County News-Herald*, March 21, 1935, p.1.

11. Interview with Lois Dalbec Sundin, April 9, 2008.

12. "Val Dalbec New Mayor," *Cook County News-Herald*, December 8, 1938, p.1.

13. Pete's Shell Service Quits Business," *Cook County News-Herald*, November 1,1971, p.1.

14. Advertisement in *Cook County News-Herald*, September 4,1958, p.2.

15. Advertisement in *Cook County News-Herald*, September 13,1958, p.5.

16. Book 194, Deed Record, p. 154, Document # 89169, Recorded February 23, 2000, Recorders Office, Cook County Court House, Grand Marais, MN.

17. Recorded as Document # 2944, June 9, 1945, Warranty Deed, Recorders Office, Cook County Court House, Grand Marais, MN.

18. Recorded as Document # 2637, September 22, 1941, Warranty Deed, Recorders Office, Cook County Court House, Grand Marais, MN.

19. Recorded as Document # 2636, September 22, 1941, Warranty Deed, Recorders Office, Cook County Court House, Grand Marais, MN.

20. Book 4, Deed Record, p. 480, Recorded February 27, 1926, Recorders Office, Cook County Court House, Grand Marais, MN.

21. Book 2, Quit Claim Deed Record, p. 149, Recorded November 14, 1925, Recorders Office, Cook County Court House, Grand Marais, MN.

22. Book 2, Quit Claim Deed Record, p. 267, Recorded August 16, 1924, Recorders Office, Cook County Court House, Grand Marais, MN.

23. "Sid Kluck Dies In California," *Cook County News-Herald*, January 21, 1954, p.1.

24. Interview with Lil Anderson, Eddie's Wife, on July 1, 2008.

25. "Dock Building, Oldest Landmark Destroyed by Fire Monday Morning," *Cook County News-Herald*, March 29. 1956, p.1.

26. "Viren Brothers Building Trading Post and Vets Clinic, " *Cook County News-Herald*, February 25, 1971, p.1.

27. "Lake Superior Trading Post Now Open," *Cook County News-Herald*, June 24, 1971, p.1.

28. "Lake Superior Trading Post Purchased By G. Marais Men," *Cook County News-Herald*, April 26, 1973, p.1.

29. "Ownership Change in Local Business, *Cook County News-Herald*, September 26, 1974, p.1.

30. "Obituaries. Richard L. Humphrey," *Cook County News-Herald*, March 25, 1982, p. 4.

31. “New Pizza Parlor Opens,” *Cook County News-Herald*, February 10, 1983, p. 4.

32. Interview with Roy Steinbrecker, October 22, 2007.

33. “Trading Post Was 'Dayton's of the North Shore.'” *Cook County News-Herald*, May 16, 1988, pp. 1 and 16..

34. “Midway building destroyed by fire,” *Cook County News-Herald*, January 25, 1988, p.1.

35. “Construction begins on new Lake Superior Trading Post,” *Cook County News-Herald*, December 26, 1988, p.1.

Chapter 9

Other Buildings and Businesses on Wisconsin Street

Introduction

After completing the research and writing about the properties in the previous chapters of this book it dawned on me that I had included a lot of the history of Wisconsin Street which runs from Highway 61 on the west end of downtown to The East Bay on the east end of town. By this time I had also collected quite a bit of information about several other buildings and businesses on this street. Consequently it seemed fitting to include a chapter on the remaining buildings and businesses that are not covered or mentioned in preceding chapters. The historical details of these properties are purposely not as complete, as they are for the businesses covered in the previous chapters. Nevertheless, the photos and information add a great deal to the historical record of Grand Marais. A few of the smaller buildings that existed during the first three decades of last century are included in some pictures in this chapter and in Chapter 10; however, very little information is included about these buildings because much of the information is lost to time. The buildings and businesses are presented in a west to east order.

Johnson's Trading Post

Charles J. Johnson began construction of his first trading post in the fall of 1906. The original building was designed to be a cross shaped structure, with "each of the four extensions being about 30 feet square, opening off a lobby in the center of the same size."[1] Johnson soon moved his office from the Cook County State Bank building into the new structure. Thus the building became primary office space for the Cook County Manufacturing Company, the Grand Marais Dock Company, and the Grand Marais Realty Company.[2] By the end of the year Johnson had also arranged for the Post Office to move into the building. Within a year Johnson had added some confectionary goods, some groceries and general merchandise to the post. The building also became a place for the buying of furs and hides. This seems to have been especially true between October 8, 1919, and July 21, 1921. During this period advertisement for hides appeared every week in the local newspaper.

Trading Post Advertisement in *Cook County News-Herald* June 16, 1920. p. 4.

In a historical article in the local newspaper in 1954, the author stated that the original trading post was destroyed by fire. The implication being that the fire took place in 1919 or 1920.[3] In this same article the author states, "The main part of the [second] building was erected in 1920, but since then many alterations have been made."[4] I was unable to find any other reference to a fire destroying the trading post about 1919 or 1920. However, it is certain that the trading post did burn down in August of 1926.

In studying various photos of the trading post it seems possible that what was some times referred to as the second trading post was in reality a major remodeling of the original building prior to 1920. It is clear from old photos of the building that an east wing off the main entrance area was added to the original building prior to 1919. It is also clear that the original logs were either replaced or covered over with what looks like cedar slabs about 1920. Various old

The Original Johnson's Trading Post. It was located on current site of the Johnson Heritage Building. *Circa 1911. (Photo courtesy of Cook County Historical Society. Photo.)*

Johnson's Trading Post. Note what looks like an addition to the right and the larger window in left wing. The steeple of the Lutheran Church is in the background. *Circa 1917. (Photo courtesy of Duane Johnson, son of Bev Johnson and grandson of Van Johnson.)*

Trading Post that burned down in August 1926.[6] Note the difference in the siding, the wider entry door and larger front window in comparison to the previous photos. The wall around the windows also look thicker which supports the theory that a layer of slabs or half logs was added to the front of the building. *(Photo courtesy of Cook County Historical Society.)*

The Second or Third Trading Post. The building was built in 1926 and torn down in 1989. *Circa 1980. (Postcard courtesy of Bill and Beth Blank.)*

The Johnson Heritage Post built on the site of the previous Trading Posts. *2008.*

photos of the trading post also indicate that the window and door openings were altered at least once. From the information available to me it is my conclusion that the original trading post was not destroyed by fire prior to 1920.

Over the years a wide range of merchandise was sold in the first building. By the time a new building was constructed in 1926, the fur trade had pretty much disappeared and the post became more of a tourist center with many of Mrs. Anna Johnson's paintings adorning the walls.[5] Eventually the second building, or perhaps it was the third, became a gift shop. The building was torn down in 1989. [7]

The foundation of the new building was put in during 1989 and the building was built in 1990. The log shell was built by Mike and Laurie Senty, owners of Log Craft Unlimited and Glen Peterson did the inside carpentry work. Lloyd K. Johnson, son of Charlie Johnson, donated the land to the Cook County Historical Society and also gave the society a gift of $350,000 to construct the new building. In addition he pledged $25,000 a year for five years for operating expenses of the building. Part of the building is used for a permanent display of Anna Johnson's art work. Anna was Lloyd's mother and Charlie's wife. The remainder of the building is used primarily for an art gallery and office space.[8]

The Grand Marais State Bank Building

The Grand Marais State Bank received its charter on August 28, 1916,[9] and opened on October 9, in temporary quarters in the Trading Post Building, while its new building was being built.[10] The bank soon moved into the first portion of the building pictured below. The officers of the new bank were: Mr. H. B. Postlewaite, President, J.A. Kirkwood, Jr., Vice President, A.M. Anderson, cashier and board members P.E. Alm, Jas. G. Scott, Wm. Clinch and L.H. Lien.[11] Louis Engelson, who was married to

Left to right on north side of Wisconsin Street: Johnson's Trading Post, Grand Marais State Bank, Chet Boisvert's Barber Shop and Soderberg Building after it was moved. The Standard Station is in the foreground. The building in front of the tanks was the new station built in 1950. The building to the right of the tanks is the storage building for gas and oil barrels and supplies for the bulk operation. 1951. The photo is an enlarged portion of an aerial view. *(Photo courtesy of Lois Pedersen Sundin.)*

a sister of James Scott, followed Postlewaite as president in 1920 and 1921.[12] In about 1922, James G. Scott was elected president of the bank and served in that capacity until his sudden death in 1947.[13] A. M. Anderson, who was married to a sister of James Scott, became the next president of the bank. From the beginning of the bank he had been the primary on site managing officer of the business.[14]

In January 1947, Richard I. Anderson, the son of A. M. Anderson joined the bank as a Vice President. He had graduated from Pennsylvania Military College in 1942 with a degree in business administration. Following graduation he entered the U.S. Army as a lieutenant and served seven months in the occupation forces in Germany prior to being discharged in 1946. Following his discharge Richard attended the United States Fidelity & Casualty Insurance School in Baltimore, Maryland.[15] After Richard joined the bank, A. M. Anderson turned over much of the management of the bank to him. This transition was interrupted during the early fifties when Richard was recalled to active military duty during the Korean War.

A few years prior to A. M. Anderson's retirement in January 1960, Richard I. Anderson became the bank president.[16] He remained as the president until 1983 when the bank was sold to V. H. Bancorp, a bank holding company. Michael LaVigne has been the president since the sale.

The first addition to the original bank building was made sometime prior to 1937.[17] The middle set of windows in the picture identify the first addition to the building. A second addition was added to the building in 1972.[18] This addition can be identified by the blue awning in the picture. In

The old bank building currently called the Gunflint Tavern on the Lake and the Superior Design Jewelry Store on the right. *July 2008*.

September of 1997, the bank moved to its new location on Highway 61. Shortly after the bank relocated the building was sold to Mr. and Mrs. James Brillhart. They remodeled the building into a mini-mall called the Fire Weed Commons and soon had six small business tenants. Jeff and Susan Gecas were the first new tenants when they started the Gunflint Tavern on the Lake. In 2003, Jeff and Susan Gecas purchased the building and during the next four years took over the entire building as other tenants either went out of business or relocated. In addition to the Gunflint Tavern Mr. and Mrs. Gecas manage the Raven Lounge, which is located in the building.

Boisvert's Barber Shop Building

The building adjacent to the bank was built in 1937 by Chester "Chet" Boisvert. Chet had his barbershop on the east side of the first floor and used the second floor for his family living area.[19] The west side of the first floor was apparently rented out to other small businesses over the years.

In October 1960, Ernie and Shirley Olson purchased the building. They lived upstairs for a few years, while Ernie had a radio and TV repair shop in the west side of the first floor. They rented out the east side of the first floor as a barbershop. At least three other men have been barbers in the building after Chet Boisvert. They were Jim Nelson, Jim Featherstone and Chuck Petek.

First Jim Nelson and Jim Featherstone worked together in the building. Then Jim Nelson left to become a pilot, leaving Featherstone alone in the building. In about 1970, Chuck Petek moved his barber business from the Arrowhead Hotel into the building and shared the first floor space with Featherstone. After a few years Featherstone moved to Minneapolis and Chuck remained alone in the first floor of the building until he moved his shop in about 1981 to his new location on First Avenue West.[20] After Ernie discontinued his radio and TV shop he rented the space to his brother for an apartment for a few years.

Stephan Hogland purchased the building on July 12, 1988. Prior to this date the building had been vacant for a few years. Stephan completely gutted and refinished the whole building bringing it back to its original luster. Stephan uses the lower level for his jewelry business called Superior Design and Jewelry and the second floor for personal living quarters or rental space.[21]

The Attic Gift Shop

The history of the Attic gift shop goes back to a building called the Common Ground, which was located on the current site of the Grand Marais State Bank on Highway 61. In this building Mrs. Bette McDonald managed a restaurant on the main floor and a gift shop in the attic for Bruce and Sue Kerfoot, who had purchased the building in about 1980. The gift shop was called the Artisans Attic. In 1984, the Kerfoots sold the building and business to Arnie Hill with the stipulation that they would retain the use of the attic for their gift shop, which Bette McDonald was to manage. This gave Bette, who had worked

The Attic Gift Shop, Crooked Spoon Cafe and White Pine North Gift Shop. *July 2008.*

for the Kerfoots for several years, continued employment after the building was sold.

The new owners of the Common Ground soon ran into financial trouble and literally abandoned the business in the middle of a night in 1985. This left Bette and the Kerfoots with a gift shop in an attic of a closed restaurant building. This forced them to look around town for a new location for the gift shop. At about the same time the local American Legion Post had purchased the former Gamble Hardware Store building on First Avenue West and vacated its building on Wisconsin Street. The Kerfoots purchased the vacated Legion building and transferred the gift shop to the building and shortened the business name to the Attic. Bette continued to managed the shop. A year later in 1986, Bette purchased the building and business from the Kerfoots. In 2005, she sold the business and building to Tom and Barbara Rawitzer.[22]

Prior to the local American Legion Post owning the building the Northern Lights Bar and Lounge was located in the building at least as far back as the early 1940's. For a number of years in the late 1920's and early 1930, the place was known as Andy's Pool Hall. In May 1935, Mrs. Agnes Jackson, started a restaurant in the back of the pool hall. Agnes was married to Archie Jackson, who was a brother to Helen Jackson, who owned Jackson's Cafe next door. In August 1935, George Brisson purchased the business and it became Brisson's Pool Hall.[23] With the change in ownership, Mrs. Magne Amdal was hired to take over the restaurant in the rear of the pool hall.[24]

The Crooked Spoon Cafe

The Crooked Spoon Cafe opened in August 2006, in the building that since 1924 had been known as Jackson's Cafe. The transitions from Jackson's Cafe began in 2005 when Jim and Jackie Larson purchased the cafe from Esther Jackson. After extensive remodeling of the building they leased the space out to Nathan and Sara Hingos who opened the Crooked Spoon Cafe in August 2006.

The history of the cafe goes back to August 1, 1923, when Helen G. Jackson purchased from Louis Falk the south 120 feet of the lot on which the cafe now stands. It is reasonable to assume that Helen began construction of the first phase of the cafe shortly thereafter. Part of the rationale for this view is the fact that Helen borrowed $3,510.00 from the Grand Marais State Bank with the lot as collateral on August 1, 1923. In addition, I found no evidence of a building on the lot prior to 1923, and following the 1908 fire that destroyed all the buildings on the south side of Wisconsin Street between First Avenue West and Broadway.

There is some evidence that Helen's father,

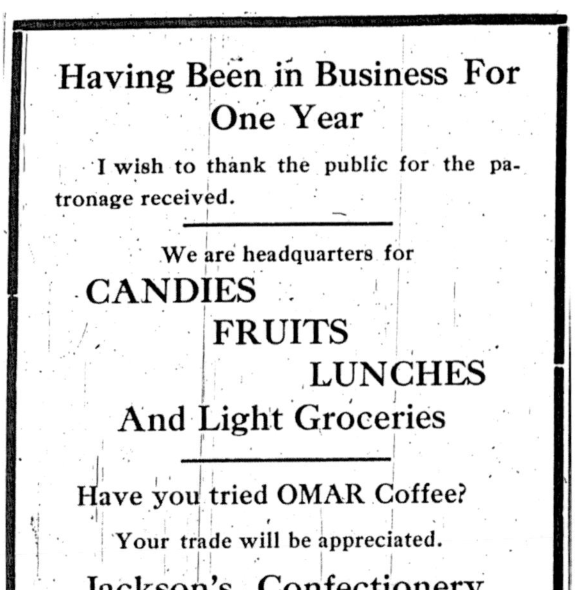

Having Been in Business For One Year

I wish to thank the public for the patronage received.

We are headquarters for

CANDIES
FRUITS
LUNCHES
And Light Groceries

Have you tried OMAR Coffee?

Your trade will be appreciated.

Jackson's Confectionery

Advertisement in *Cook County News-Herald,* August 30, 1916, p. 8.

Fred Jackson Sr. assisted her in getting established in the cafe business. At the time he was operating a small cafe called Jackson's Confectionery in a small building in the back

Jackson's Cafe and Bus Stop. *Circa 1950. (Photo courtesy of the Cook County Historical Museum.)*

or north end of the lot Helen had purchased. He had opened this business in August 1915, in a building he was renting from Louis Falk. Fred discontinued his confectionery and cafe venture when Helen opened her cafe.

In about 1926, Jackson's Cafe became the Greyhound Bus stop. A year later Helen added an area to the back of her building that originally was to be a small theater that would hold about twenty people. The theater never came to be and the added space became part of an expanded cafe.[25]

On February 9, 1939, Helen's brother Fred R. Jackson Jr. and his wife Esther purchased the cafe from her estate.[26] For a short time Fred and Esther Jackson leased the cafe out to others. For example, in February 1946, they leased the cafe out to Mr. and Mrs. Frank Rosener,[27] and a year later to Mr. and Mrs. Frank Barnard.[28]

During the 1970's, Jackson's Cafe became the county location for purchasing licenses for vehicles, boats, and trailers. During this period and the decade of the 1990's, the cafe part of the business gradually diminished. About the year 2000, the Happy Times Bus Company of Thunder Bay transferred the bus stop to the Blue Water Cafe. The Greyhound Bus Company had discontinued service to Grand Marais many years earlier. In about 2003, Esther closed the cafe because of her failing health. Her husband Fred had passed away in the mid-1980's.

The Shore Theater

In July 1937, Loren Leng began construction of the Shore Theater, on vacant lots next to what is now the Blue Water Cafe.[29] The theater, which had a capacity of 310 people, opened in October of the same year. There was an apartment on the second floor of the building and small rooms on both sides of the main entrance on the first floor, which

Left to right: Tony's Lunch, Shore Theater and Du Nord Cafe. *Circa 1954. (Photo courtesy of Charles Humphrey.)*

were available for rent.[30] Louisa Humphrey, a sister of Milford Humphrey, rented the first floor room west of the entrance from 1946[31] through December 1955 for a shop called the Louisa Gift Shop.[32] There was also a barbershop for a while in the left front window area of the theater. The theater closed in 1968.

The Cook County State Bank

The Cook County State Bank was chartered in September 1901, and opened in October in Johnson's Mercantile Company building. The original shareholders were Charlie J. Johnson with 47 shares, B. C. Taylor with 47 shares, General E. M. Pope with 3 shares and H. C. Koerner with 3 shares.[33] The original bank building was destroyed in the October 12, 1908 fire. In July 1904, General Pope sold his stock in the bank to Charles Johnson, and A. V. Johnson was

Wisconsin Street. Left to right: Grand Hotel, uncertain of name of building or business, Charlie Johnson's Grand Marais Mercantile Company and the Cook County State Bank, The building in the far right is the Broadway Hotel. *Circa 1905. (Photo courtesy of Cook County Historical Society.)*

New Cook County State Bank built of concrete or concrete blocks. John Lundin's house on the left. *1910. (Photo courtesy of Cook County Historical Museum.)*

elected as cashier in the bank.[34] A new concrete bank building was built shortly after the fire.

In July 1916, L. G. Lundquist and his brother G. F. Lundquist took over the management of the bank. G. F. Lundquist was formerly with the First State Bank of Strandberg, South Dakota, and L. G. Lundquist had lived in Grand Marais for three years.[35] In October 1921, the bank was consolidated into the Grand Marais State Bank. The Lundquist brothers retired from the bank at the time and the officers at the Grand Marais State Bank remained the same.[36]

In 1921, John Rindal had a tailoring shop on the second floor of the bank building.[37]

Wisconsin Street Looking West from Broadway. The sign on the bank building reads "News Herald." The newspaper's office was on the second floor. *Circa 1914. (Photo courtesy of Cook County Historical Museum.)*

Cook County State Bank Building and Bramer Building on Wisconsin Street. *Circa 1921. (Photo courtesy of Cook County Historical Museum.)*

A View of Wisconsin Street looking west. The building on the left is the Toftey Store. The Bramer Building is on the right on the north side of Wisconsin Street. The left sign on the Bramer building reads Groceries, Meats & Gen'l MDSE The sign on the right read Ladies & Gents Furnishing. Next to the Bramer Building is the Cook County State Bank. The one story building to the left of the Bank is Joe Schoen Confectionery Store. The two story building on the left is the original Court House Building, which was moved to this site. At the time of this picture the building housed J. W. Schoen's Theatre. *Circa 1915. (Photo courtesy off Cook County Historical Museum.)*

The Old Court House Building and Confectionary Store

The old court house building was moved to its new location on Wisconsin Street in April 1913[38] from the location of the new Court House, which was completed in 1912. Fred Bramer had purchased the building from the county and hired Andrew Hedstrom to move it for him.[39] Sometime during the next few years Joe Schoen purchased the building from Fred Bramer. In August 1914, Joe Schoen purchased the confectionary business from George Brisson and leased the Brisson building, which was the one story building east of the relocated court house building.[40] By April 1919, Joe Schoen had remodeled the old court house building into a "New Moving Picture Theatre." To launch his new theatre he ran ads in the local paper in April giving away a "Season Ticket" to the person suggesting the best name for the new moving picture theatre.[41]

The old Court House Building and the small one story building beside it were located where Sven and Ole's Pizza business is today. In February 1920, fires destroyed the Schoen's theatre and confectionery store and Woods and Seglem's barber shop and billiard hall which was adjacent and west of the theater. The Cook County State Bank building was also badly burned.[42]

A view of Wisconsin Street from the west. Additional details can be seen when enlarged. On the left side of the picture left to right are: John Lundin's Store, a pool hall and/or Woods & Seglem's Barbershop. The building with a peaked roof is the original courthouse building, which housed Joe Schoen's Theatre. Next is a small one story building housing Schoen's Confectionery Store. The two story bank building with a sign that states "News Herald," and the Bramer Building. On the right is the Toftey Store, then what appears to be a barber shop, then a small store or cafe building, and then the Hotel Paine. Note wooden sidewalk on right side of street. *Circa 1914. (Photo courtesy of Cook County Historical Museum.)*

A report of a fire in 1929 indicates that the reference to a small store or cafe building in the above photo caption referred to the Community Restaurant.[43]

The Bramer Building

The Bramer building on the corner was built in 1911 by C. O. Backlund and Andrew Hedstrom.[44] Ed Nunstedt and John Winger in July 1915, bought out Fred Bramer's dry goods, shoes and clothing store and Fred Bramer's interest in the Johnson and Bramer grocery store, which were located in the building.[45] Starting in about 1916, a company called The Northern Furniture Co. was housed in the second floor of the building. In addition to furniture this store sold items such as toys, clocks, dishes, lamps, phonographs and records.[46] George Leng purchased the Bramer Building sometime prior to March 28, 1929.[47]

The U.S. Post Office was located in the east side of the building, from sometime during the 1920's until 1957. In 1957, the Post Office moved to its new building on the northeast corner of Highway 61 and 1st Avenue West, the current location of the Arrowhead Pharmacy. In 1929 or 1930, Arthur L. E. Peterson, a pharmacist and Dr. W. R. Smith moved to Grand Marais from Dawson, Minnesota. Arthur Peterson had been working in his father's drug store in Dawson and Dr. Smith had been practicing medicine for about a year in the town. Dr. Smith had grown up in Duluth and part of what prompted him to move to Grand Marais was the prospect of cooler summers than he experienced in Dawson.[48] Upon moving to Grand Marais Peterson opened the Peterson Drug Store on the first floor and west side of the Leng Building. The first location of Dr. Smith's office was behind the drug store on the first floor.[49]

For living quarters when they arrived in Grand Marais, the Peterson and Smith families moved into apartments on the second floor of the Leng building. Arthur Peterson and his family lived in the apartment on the east side of the stairway. Dr. Smith and his family lived in the apartment on the west side of the stairway. The back part of the upstairs area in the building was unfinished at this time.[50] In about 1934, the Smiths and Petersons purchased lots in Grand Marais, built homes on them and moved out of the apartments. Then Dr. Smith moved his medical practice office to the west side apartment area on the second floor where he maintained his office until he retired in 1975.[51] In July 1937, Dr. Harry Pratt, a dentist, moved his practice from St. Paul to the second floor of the building.[52] Dr. Smith and Dr. Pratt shared a common waiting room, between their offices, for their patients. In the late 1940's, Dr. Pratt moved his practice to a building on 1st Avenue West.

In 1938, Arthur Peterson rented one side of the new CO-OP building on 1st Avenue West and moved his Rexall Drug store there. After the drug store moved out, Earl Leng, one of the sons of George Leng, opened Leng's Fountain in the space formerly occupied by the drug store.

In the early 1940's, George Leng moved into the upstairs apartment closest to Wisconsin Street. His wife had died in 1936. At various times, rooms on the east side were rented out

Wisconsin Street looking west. The Toftey Grocery and Hardware Store is on the left. On the right side of the photo is the Leng's Building, followed by an open space where Frank Cherry's Bakery and before that the Cook County State Bank once was located. The next building is Becky's Hardware Store and then Humphrey's. *Circa 1941. (The photo is a portion of post card courtesy of Bill and Beth Blank.)*

Businesses on right side of Wisconsin Street. Left to right: Leng's, Becky's Hardware, Humphrey's, Jackson's Cafe, a Tavern and Peter Alm's Store. Note the two-story addition to Leng's building where the Cook County State Bank had been located. This building was built in approximately 1952. *Circa 1953. (Postcard courtesy of Bill and Beth Blank.)*

for office use. For many years Dr. Smith used a room for his x-ray equipment. During the 1950's, George Johnson, an attorney, rented the back room on the east side for an office and for a few years a geological survey staff rented a room. In recent years the second floor has been used for expanded retail space for The Market and for storage space.

Between 1952 and 1954, George and Earl Leng constructed a two-story building adjacent to their building in the space where the Cook County Bank

An enlargement of a portion of the above postcard. Note: Joynes Ben Franklin Store had not been built yet. *Circa 1953. (Postcard courtesy of Bill and Beth Blank.)*

Postcard of Wisconsin Street looking west from Broadway. *Circa 1955.*

was once located. In July 1955, the fountain business was transferred to this new building. The back wall of the store contained a 20-foot magazine display rack.[53]

During the winter of 1960-1961, the space where Leng's Fountain had been located was remodeled, and in the spring of 1961, Mrs. Loren (Irene) Leng opened a gift shop in this space.[54] During the 1960's, Bobbie Johnson and Rita Portner rented the space where the Post Office had been located for their clothing store called the Villager.

Over the years the gift shop expanded to the entire first floor of the building and became known as Leng's Market or The Market.

The Leng Market on the right. Moose Tracks, a "T" shirt and sweatshirt store in the previous site of Leng's Fountain. The portion in blue is the Market. *2008*

Currently Beth Schroeder, the daughter of Loren and Irene Leng and granddaughter of George Leng, manages The Market.

In recent years the Leng's Fountain building has been leased to others and since about 2005 has been converted to a store called Moose Tracks that sells clothing such as "T" shirts and sweatshirts.

Sven & Ole's Pizza Site

In the night of March 21, 1929, or early morning of March 22, a fire started in the Nyland's Barber Shop, which was located to the left of the People's Supply Company building. The fire soon spread to the People's Supply Company and then to Frank Cherry's Bakery. Cherry's Bakery was in the remodeled or perhaps rebuilt building, which formerly housed the Cook County State Bank. From the Cherry Bakery the fire spread to the Bramer Building, on the corner of Wisconsin Street and Broadway. At the time the building belonged to George Leng and housed the Post Office.[56]

The owners of the People's Supply Store rebuilt the store following the fire. On January 6, 1941, Hilmer "Becky" Becklund purchased the building and business and renamed the place "Becky's" and opened a

People's Supply Store on Wisconsin Street. The words on the awning read Hardware, People's Supply and Groceries. Frank Cherry's Bakery is on the right. *1928. (Photo courtesy of Cook County Historical Museum.)*

Becky's. C.O. Backlund and Sons. The sign on the left reads Hardware and Sporting Goods and the sign on the right reads Plumbing and Building Supplies. *Circa 1955. (Photo courtesy of Terry Backlund.)*

grocery store in the building. In April 1942, Becky rented a section of the building to I. J. Sawvell who opened a Gamble Store in his space.[57] In October of 1942, Becky's father, C. O. Backlund took over the building and the grocery business and combined it with his construction business.[58] The grocery side of the store became C. O's. Meat and Grocery. In a few years Becky's name was dropped from the title.

C.O. Backlund and Sons Hardware Store. The sign on the left reads Hardware Plumbing and the sign on right reads Building Supplies. The sign on the next building is for Leng's Soda Fountain and the Coop Store is in the background. *Circa 1960, (Photo courtesy of Terry Backlund.)*

I. J. Sawvell ownership of the Gamble Store lasted just over two years. We know this because in August 1944, E. R. Bushman ran his first advertisement as owner of the Gamble Store. He apparently purchased the business from I. J. Sawvell prior to this date. In less than a year, in July 1945, E. R. Bushman moved the Gamble Store to the former location of LeSage's Cafe on 1st Avenue West. This is the current location of the Grand Marais American Legion.[59] Sometime after the Gamble Store had moved out of their building, C. O. Backlund and Sons converted the entire building into a hardware, plumbing and building supply store.

Sven and Ole's Pizza. *June 2009.*

In November 1972, the ownership of the business changed to Backlund Hardware, Inc., a corporation owned by C.O. Backlund and Sid Backlund Sr. as equal partners. About this same time they discontinued the retail hardware business. The C. O. Backlund and Sons Construction business continued to operate at their location east of town. At this same time the east side of the store was rented out to a business called Robinson's Clothing and Fabric Store. Following C. O. Backlund's death in 1975, his grandsons Sid Jr. and Terry Backlund each inherited one-fourth of the building.

On July 30, 1981, Sid Jr. and Terry Backlund, started a small business selling nachos, popcorn, hotdogs, their Mom's brownies and pop on the front and left side of the store. In the fall they added pieces of pizza to their takeout business before closing for the winter. The right side of the store continued to be rented out as a clothing and fabric store.

When the summer of 1982 arrived, Sid Jr. and Terry re-opened their business and it has remained open year around since. In the fall of 1985, they expanded into the space, which had been rented out, and in 1987, they added the Pickle Herring Club to the business. On February 1, 1995, Sid Jr. and Terry became the sole owners of the building by purchasing their parents share of the real estate. In 1998 Terry moved to Minneapolis to pursue other business interests and in 2001, he sold his share of the partnership to his brother Sid Jr.[60]

The World's Best Donuts

In the summer of 1969, Merieta Engel and Irma Toftey started the Donut Shop in a small building at the intersection of Highway 61 and 5th Avenue West that is now a part of

The First Donut Shop. *1969. (Photo courtesy of Dee Brazell.)*

The Second Location of the Donut Shop. *Circa 1970's. (Photo courtesy of Dee Brazell.)*

the Dock Side Fish Market. They made the donuts in the basement and sold them on the street level area of the building.

After about a month and a-half in their first location they had to relocate because a health inspector said the premises did not meet the health department codes. Therefore, Irma and Merieta moved the Donut Shop to the east side of what had been Joynes Federated Store, and earlier the P. A. Alm General Merchandise Store. In 1978, Irma sold her share of the business to Merieta.

In 1978, Sherrie Lindskog became a partner in the business with her mother. In 1983 until 1988, another daughter of Merieta, Donna Wilson, became a partner in the business. Dee and Stacey, the daughters of Chester and Sherrie Lindskog, who had worked in the business since they were little girls, purchased the business and building in 2002 from their mother and grandmother. The first phase of the building on the current location was built in 1978. The seating area on the east side was added in 1983. In January, 2010, Dee and Stacy purchased the land on which the building stands from Joan Drury, who also owns the Drury Lane Book Store east of the Donut Shop.

The World's Best Donuts. The Cook County Historical Museum is in the background. *July 2008.*

The Ed Toftey store was built in 1913[61] and razed in 1958.[62] *1935. (Photo courtesy of Cook County Historical Society.)*

IGA Foodliner Store. This store was built in 1958. *Circa 1959. (Photo courtesy Cook County Historical Museum.)*

The Security State Bank located on the site of the former IGA Foodliner Store. The bank opened as Cook County State Bank on October 3, 1994 and became a branch of Security State Bank of Aitkin, Minnesota on June 22, 2001. *July 2008*

The Security State Bank Corner

Mr. and Mrs. Gene Lashinski purchased the IGA store in 1978. The store burned down in November 1989 and the Lashinskis opened a new IGA store on Highway 61 in June 1990.

A Copy of a Painting by Theodora Brown in 1981 of the Pioneer House Gift Shop. *(Photo Courtesy of Nancy Dalbec.)*

Drury Lane Books

The complete history of this building we do not know, but we do know that the history of this house involves Edward Wakelin and the Mayhew family. It was once the home of George Mayhew, the son of Joseph E. Mayhew, the first lighthouse keeper in Grand Marais.[63] George Mayhew was the first non-Indian baby to be born in Cook County.

On February 24, 1896, Edward Wakelin sold Lots number 1 and 2 on which the above building and the Donut Shop are located, to Nicholas Probeck for $200.[64] A few months later on November 21, 1896, Probeck sold one-half undivided interest in the lots to Joseph E. Mayhew.[65] Wakelin, Probeck and Joseph Mayhew were all unmarried at the time of these transactions. Four years later on January 22, 1900, Probeck sold Mayhew his other interest in the lots.[66]

In 1914, the property was foreclosed and a sheriff sale took place. Through a series of transactions, too detailed for the purposes of this book, Joseph E. Mayhew, and ultimately his son, George Mayhew ended up owning the two lots.

On August 19, 1952, Mrs. Helen Dalbec purchased the house from the estate of George H. Mayhew. For a few years Mrs. Dalbec managed a gift shop in the building, which she called the Pioneer House Gift Shop. In the late 1970's and early 1980's, someone rented the building for a shoe repair store. From 1982 to 2001, Jan Sivertson rented

The Drury Lane Books Store. Located east of the Donut Shop and across the street from the East Bay Suites. *September 2008.*

the building and called the place Sivertson Gallery.[67] In 1974, Helen gave one-half of her interests in the property to her daughter Nancy. In 1989, Nancy received additional interest in the property and Helen's other daughter, Lois Dalbec Pedersen, received part interest in the property. In March 2002, they sold the property to Joan Drury (via the corporate name Drury Lane Books, LLC.) Joan promptly remodeled the house and opened the Drury Lane Books store.

Conclusion

Throughout the history of Cook County, Grand Marais has been a major focal point. When the town first emerged and until modern roads were constructed, the Grand Marais harbor was the major entry point for people and goods to Cook County. Not only was the natural harbor a good place for ships to load and unload; the town was also centrally located between the end of the Gunflint Trail on the north, the Canadian Border on the east, and the Lake County line on the west end of the county.

Today Grand Marais is the location of the county government, the county school system, the county hospital, the public library, the Sawtooth Clinic and numerous services and businesses. Furthermore, it is the only organized city or village in Cook County.

The economy of the town has always been closely tied to the economy of the entire county. One way to view the economy of Grand Marais and Cook County from a historical, as well as a contemporary perspective, is to identify the three to seven major sources of jobs and contributors to construction projects. These are the economic pillars of the local economy. Around 1900, the major pillars were lumbering, mining and railroad interests with three smaller pillars involving farming, commercial fishing, governmental entities and tourism. From roughly 1900 to 1950, the impact of farming and commercial fishing on the economy increased and then declined. During the depression years, (the 1930's) the economic impact of the government via CCC, WPA and PWA programs was very significant. During the second half of the past century the Taconite Harbor and the railroad to the harbor became a significant pillar in the county economy.

Over the past one hundred years the economic impact of the above-mentioned pillars has been reversed. Today the two big economic pillars in the county are tourism and governmental entities, with lumbering, Taconite Harbor and the railroad being smaller pillars, and farming and commercial fishing very small pillars. All of these pillars create jobs and the need for a variety of supporting businesses such as grocery stores, barber shops and gas stations that also contribute to the economy, but these businesses couldn't exist without the major economic pillars.

The pillar of tourism includes the businesses that cater to tourists, i.e. the resorts, restaurants, motels, golf courses, gift shops, ski areas, canoe outfitters and others. The pillar called governmental entities includes a wide range of jobs and money for constructing such things as highways, harbors, schools, office buildings and more. On the federal level Cook County benefits by the presence of the U.S. Forest Service, the Coast Guard, Border Patrol, Customs, Immigration, the Grand Portage National Monument, U. S. Army Corp of Engineers and the Bureau of Indian Affairs. On the state level the county benefits from highway construction, maintenance and policing, four state parks, state forest land, game management and the support of public schools with state funding. On the local level, we have the county highway department, the public school system, the county hospital and care center and the city government in Grand Marais. All these governmental entities represent a significant portion of the total local monthly payroll with much of the money coming from outside the county.

It is also worth noting that Cook County is the twelfth largest county out of eighty-seven in the state and has the lowest or next to lowest population of all the counties. In addition, various levels of government own approximately 91 percent of the county land. This percentage figure excludes the Grand Portage Reservation. These factors help make the county a very interesting place in which to live and to visit. Within this milieu, the population of Grand Marais, over the years, has remained at approximately one-third of that of the county as a whole.

This concludes a short history of a portion of Grand Marais and parts of Cook County. It has been a fascinating experience doing the research for this book. At times it was hard to stop reading old newspapers. At other times it was difficult to know what to include or exclude from this volume. I have included references to much of the information that hopefully will be helpful to someone who wants to research the history of other portions of the town or county. If I have made any errors in my effort to document the history of this grand town, I hope that readers will bring them to my attention.

(Endnotes)

1. "Topics of a Week," *Cook County Herald*, October 20, 1906, p. 5.

2. "Topics of a Week," *Cook County Herald*, October 20, 1906, p. 5.

3. "Past-Plus...Present," *Cook County News-Herald*, March 11, 1954, p. 2.

4. "Trading Post Burned Friday," *Cook County News-Herald*, August 26, 1926, p. 1.

5. "Past-Plus...Present," *Cook County News-Herald*, March 11, 1954, p. 2.

6. "Trading Post Burned Friday," *Cook County News-Herald*, August 26, 1926, p. 1.

7. "Historical Society Plans to reconstruct Johnson Trading Post," *Cook County News-Herald*, January 2, 1989, p. 1.

8. "Heritage Post - Lodgepole Goes Up," *Cook County News-Herald*, June 4, 1990, p. 1.

9. "New Bank Started For Cook County," *Cook County News-Herald*, September 13, 1916, p. 1.

10. "New Bank to Open For Business Next Week," *Cook County News-Herald*, October 4, 1916, p. 1

11. "Grand Marais State Bank Advertisement," *Cook County News-Herald*, October 11, 1916, p. 8.

12. "Grand Marais State Bank," *Cook County News-Herald*, July 14, 1921.

13. "JAS. G. SCOTT DIES AT 66," *Cook County News-Herald*, January 16, 1947, p. 1

14. Interview with Richard Anderson, October 21, 2008.

15. "Bank Elects For Year; R. Anderson New Director," *Cook County News-Herald*, January 9, 1947, p. 1.

16. "A.M. Anderson Retires as Banker," *Cook County News-Herald*, January 14, 1960, p. 1.

17. Interview with Richard Anderson, July 9, 2008.

18. "Bank Addition Progressing Toward June 1 Completion," *Cook County News-Herald*, March 30, 1972, p. 1.

19. Some of the New Buildings Completed During Year." *Cook County News-Herald*, December 23, 1937, p. 1.

20. Interview with Chuck Petek, Sept. 9, 2008.

21. Interview with Stephan Hogland, September 26, 2008.

22. Interview with Bette McDonald, August 12, 2008.

23. Advertisement "Change in Management," *Cook County News-Herald*, August 15, 1935, p.4.

24. Advertisement, "Change in Management," *Cook County News-Herald*, August 15, 1935, p.4.

25. Interview with Stuart Jackson, September 16, 2008.

26. Book 7, Miscellaneous Record, p. 542, Recorders Office, Cook County Court House, Grand Marais, MN.

27. "Jacksons Lease Restaurant," *Cook County News-Herald*, February 7, 1946, p. 1.

28. "Jackson's Cafe Under New Management," *Cook County News-Herald*, January 9, 1947, p.1.

29. "New Theatre Now Being built," *Cook County News-Herald*, July 15, 1937, p.1.

30. "New Leng Theatre Opened Here," *Cook County News-Herald*, October 21, 1937, p.1.

31. "The Humphrey Saga," Edited by Milford Humphrey, 1993, Louisa Humphrey's article, pp. 7-8. (Mimeographed.)

32. "Going Out of Business" Advertisement, *Cook County News-Herald*, December 15, 1955, p. 3.

33. Willis H. Raff, *Pioneers In the Wilderness*, (Grand Marais, MN: Cook County Historical Society, 1981), pp. 349-350.

34. "Local Items," *Cook County Herald*, July 16, 19i04, p. 5.

35. "Local Bank Changes Hands," *Cook County News-Herald*, July 26, 1916, p. 1.

36. "Banks to Be Merged Into A Single But Stronger Institution," *Cook County News-Herald*, October 20, 1921, p. 1.

37. Advertisement, " Tailoring...John Rindal, *Cook County News-Herald*, April 28, 1921, p. 3.

38. "Topic of a Week," *Cook County News-Herald*, April 3, 1913, p. 1

39. "Topic of a Week," *Cook County News-Herald*, April 3, 1913, p. 1

40. "Topics of a Week," *Cook County News-Herald*, August 6, 1914, p.1.

41. Advertisement, *Cook County News-Herald*, April 16, 1919, p.4.

42. "Another Big Fire Saturday Forenoon," *Cook County News-Herald*, February 11, 1920, p. 1

43. "Fire Destroys Four Business Houses in Midnight Blaze," *Cook County News-Herald*, March 28, 1929, p. 1.

44. Interview with Terry Backlund, September 5, 2008.

45. "Topics of a Week," *Cook County News-Herald*, July 15, 1915, p.1.

46. "Advertisement," *Cook County News-Herald*, December 12, 1917, p. 3.

47. "Fire Destroys Four Business Houses in Midnight Blaze," *Cook County News-Herald*, March 28, 1929, p. 1.

48. Interview with Rosemary Lamson, daughter of Dr. Smith, June 5, 2009.

49. Interview with Larry Peterson, son of Arthur Peterson, June 6, 2009.

50. Interview with Larry Peterson, son of Arthur Peterson, June 1, 2009.

51. Interview with Rosemary Lamson, daughter of Dr. Smith, September 30, 2008.

52. "Dr. Pratt is New Local Dentist," *Cook County News-Herald*, July 15, 1937, p. 1.

53. Leng's Hold Open House," *Cook County News-Herald*, July 14, 1955, p. 1.

54. "Mrs. Loren Leng Buys Gift Shop," *Cook County News-Herald*, October 20, 1960, p. 1.

55. "Historical Reflections," *Cook County News-Herald*, November 9, 1987, p. 1.

56. "Fire Destroys Four Business Houses in Midnight Blaze," *Cook County News-Herald*, March 28, 1929, p. 1. and "Past Plus," *Cook County News-Herald*, October 13, 1955, p. 2.

57. "Gamble Store to hold Open Here Soon," *Cook County News-Herald*, April 9, 1942,p. 1.

58. "Advertisement for Becky's Store," *Cook County News-Herald*, October15, 1942, p. 8.

59. "Advertisement Gambles," *Cook County News-Herald*, July 5, 1945.

60. Interview with Terry Backlund, September 5, 2008.

61. "Topics of a Week," *Cook County Herald*, July 10, 1913, p.1.

62. "New Store Will Replace Toftey's Landmark," *Cook County News-Herald*, May 1, 1958, p. 1.

63. Willis H. Raff, *Pioneers in the Wilderness* (Grand Marais, MN: Cook County Historical Society, 1981), p. 38.

64. Book E, Deed Record, p. 47, Recorders Office, Cook County Court House, Grand Marais, MN.

65. Book E, Deed Record, p. 111, Recorders Office, Cook County Court House, Grand Marais, MN.

66. Book I, Deed Record, p. 518, Recorders Office, Cook County Court House, Grand Marais, MN.

67. Interview with Jan Sivertson, November 3, 2008.

Chapter 10

Supplemental Photos

Wisconsin Street. Left to right: John Johnson's Place, Lundin's Building, Schoen's Theater, Bramer Building, and Lakeside Hotel. Celebration of Formal Opening of Duluth-Port Arthur Highway. *August 1917. (Photo courtesy of Terry Backlund.)*

As I searched photos relating to the main focus of this book I came across information and photos that didn't fit into the previous chapters, but seemed too pertinent to leave out. Some photos are about downtown Grand Marais and some are about other areas of the city. All of them are intended to complement the material in the previous chapters and provide the reader with a more complete view of the town's history.

In August 1917, about 500 people visited Grand Marais to celebrate the opening of the Highway between Duluth and Port Arthur. The completion of the border bridge over the Pigeon River was one of the last projects in the long awaited international highway. The mayors of Port Arthur, Fort William, and Duluth were present at the celebration.

South side of Wisconsin Street. Hotel Paine on right. Celebration of Formal Opening of Duluth-Port Arthur Highway. *August 1917. (Photo courtesy of Terry Backlund.)*

Madison Street, now First Avenue West, looking North. On the left side left to right: the Motor Inn Storage Garage, The *Cook County News Herald* Newspaper building, a one story unknown building and then the Hussey Boarding House. On the right side is a building advertising tires, that later became the Chevrolet dealership. In the background is the Midway Garage building with a big sign saying "Garage Storage." *Circa 1920. (Photo courtesy of Duane Johnson. son of Bev Johnson and grandson of Van Johnson.)*

Very early downtown Grand Marais. *Circa 1903. (Photo courtesy of Cook County Historical Society.)*

In the above photo a small Chevrolet sign is attached to the front of the building and a single gas pump is located in front of the building. During the early years of cars in Grand Marais, which was approximately 1916 to 1925, it was common to rent storage space for the cars in the winter. This was due, in part, to the fact that few roads in Cook County were useable for cars in the winter at this time.

During the same month, the CO-OP opened in their new location. Shortly thereafter, Arthur L. Peterson purchased the original CO-OP building and moved his drug

The CO-OP Store when it was located on 1st Avenue West. *Circa 1938. (Photo courtesy of Cook County Historical Society.)*

The Cook County Cooperative was incorporated in June 1935.[2] At first it operated as a retail store in a temporary location, which I have not been able to locate. In September 1938, it opened in a new store building on the lot adjacent to and north of Mabel's Cafe. This is the current location of Chuck Petek's Barber Shop and the Gunflint Mercantile Store. Pentti Penttila was the manger of the store at the time.[3] In early August 1945, the CO-OP Association purchased Joe Anderson's Cash Market on the northwest corner of Broadway and Wisconsin Street.[4]

store into the property in September 1945.[5] Peterson may have been renting part of the CO-OP building for his Drug Store since the building was built.

Mrs. Mabel Bissell, had been the proprietor of an establishment called the Dew Drop Inn since about 1930. This business was located in the frame building to the left of Mabel's Cafe. In May 1935, it was announced in the local paper that she was relocating The Dew Drop Inn to "its new location, the former cabaret building," Whether she intended to

Mabel's Cafe. Located on 1st Avenue West behind Peter Alm's Store, north of Joynes parking lot, where the "T" Shirt Outfitters store is currently located. *Circa 1935. (Photo Courtesy of the Cook County Historical Society)*

keep the name of the place Drew Drop Inn or not, we do not know. We do know that her new place soon became known as Mabel's Cafe. In April 1938, the interior of the building was destroyed by fire. At the time Ed Nunstead owned the building and Mabel and her husband C. A. Hoppenstedt owned and managed the cafe business. The Hoppenstedts were able to reopen the cafe on July 2, 1938. The cafe closed in 1979.

LeSage's Cafe was established by Helga LeSage. It was in operation at least as early as 1932. On June 28, 1938, Helga married Leo Hussey and they continued to operate the business until 1945. In July 1945, E. R. Bushman, moved his Gamble Store into the building formerly known as LeSage's Cafe. Prior to this date Mr. Bushman had operated his Gamble Store business in C. O. Backlund's building on Wisconsin Street. In 1984 or 1985, the American Legion Post purchased the building.

LeSage's Cafe. Located on 1st Avenue West, where the American Legion Club is currently located. *Circa 1936. (Photo courtesy of the Cook County Historical Society.)*

The building at right is across the street from the current location of the Senior Center. Cherry's bakery moved to this location after it's building on Wisconsin burned down in March 1929.

Frank Cherry's Bakery in a new building on Broadway. *Circa 1935. (Photo courtesy of Cook County Historical Society.)*

Coast Guard Station and part of Down Town Grand Marais. *1951. (Photo courtesy of Lois Pedersen Sundin.)*

This photo is an enlarged portion of a larger photo of downtown Grand Marais. The street in the foreground is First Avenue West, then called Madison St. On the left is Broadway, the main street of that day. John Lundin's house is on the right. The big building in the middle is a livery stable. The Cook County State Bank is in the middle of the picture, and the Broadway Hotel is left of the livery stable. To the left and north of the Broadway Hotel is Fred Bramer's saloon. The small building north of the saloon is a barber shop. I was not able identify the name of the two story building north of the barber shop. The Lighthouse Keepers House is to the right of the Broadway Hotel.

Ships Loading Logs from Harbor. *Circa 1950's. (Postcard courtesy of Bill and Beth Blank.)*

Stockpiles of Logs on Point. *Circa 1953. (Postcard courtesy of Bill and Beth Blank.)*

The original Cobblestone Station, which was owned and operated by Homer Massie who lived with his family in the house on the left. The location was on Highway 61 where the Pump House Fitness Center is now located. The building on the right is the Wigwam Movie Theater. George Leng built the theater in about 1912 and called it the Princess Theater. About 1920, he changed the name to the Wigwam. The Wigwam was located approximately where the Gunflint Trail Arch is now located. *Circa 1930. (Photo courtesy of the Cook County Historical Society.)*

Shold & Lovaas Mobil Station at the intersection of Highway 61 and Broadway which is the current location of South of the Border Cafe. The business was owned and operated by Kenny Lovaas and Roger Shold. *Circa 1954. (Photo courtesy of Kenny Lovaas.)*

The Pure Station opened in 1954 and was owned by Wally Schulte. It was located on Highway 61 where Gunflint Realty is currently located. *Circa 1954. (Photo courtesy of Cook County Historical Society.)*

The Standard Station opened in 1955 on Highway 61 where the current Holiday Station is located. *Circa 1956. (Photo courtesy of Terry Backlund.)*

Two Tennis Courts Constructed in 1938 by CCC North of Court House. *1938. (Photo by Milford Humphrey, courtesy of Cook County Historical Society.)*

Originally the museum building was the official Lighthouse keeper's residence. It was built in 1896. It has been a museum since 1966. The building is on the National Registry of Historic Places. Joseph E. Mayhew, the son of Dr. Thomas Mayhew was the first resident in the building. He was Lighthouse keeper from 1886 to 1902. The addition in the rear of the building was opened in the spring of 2008.

The Cook County Historical Museum. The addition in the rear of the building opened in 2008.

(Endnotes)

1. "Formal Opening of Duluth-Port Arthur Highway Celebration with Large Attendance," *Cook County News-Herald*, August 22, 1917, p. 1.

2. "Articles of Incorporation Filed For Coop Store," *Cook County News-Herald*, June 27, 1935, p. 1.

3. "New Store Opening," *Cook County News-Herald*, September 15, 1938, p. 1.

4. "CO-OP Buys Anderson's," *Cook County News-Herald*, August 2, 1945 p. 1.

5. "Real Estate Moves in and Near Village," *Cook County News-Herald*, September 13, 1945 p. 1.

6. "New Restaurants Open For Business," *Cook County News-Herald*, May 9, 1935, p. 1.

7. "Mabel's Cafe Destroyed by Fire," *Cook County News-Herald*, April 7, 1938, p. 1.

8. "Real Estate Moves in and Near Village," *Cook County News-Herald*, September 13, 1945 p. 1.

9. "Caught On The Run," *Cook County Herald*, June 6, 1903, p. 5.

10. "Topics of a Week," *Cook County Herald*, November 5, 1904, p. 5.

Appendix

Miscellaneous Information About Grand Marais and Cook County

The following list of happenings and events were outside the primary focus of this book but seemed noteworthy. The entries are intended to complement the information in the previous pages. They are not intended to be a complete list of significant happenings. One thing that caught my attention in the list is the number of destructive fires that have occurred over the years in the town of Grand Marais. Fires mentioned earlier in the book are not listed here. The items are listed in chronological order, which helps puts things in a historical perspective.

1. Fred Bramer moved his saloon building to lot 14, block 31, just north of the Broadway Hotel in 1903.[1]

2. The first high school building was built in 1908 and dedicated on February 9, 1909. In 1910, there were two high school graduates. The first in Cook County.[2]

3. The Bramer Building, a two-story frame building on Monroe was destroyed by fire in October 1907.[3]

4. Olson Brothers' Livery burned to ground in 1920, A. Van Johnson had built the livery about 1903. The Olson Brothers had purchased the building in 1911. At the time of the fire Ertsgard and Charles Boostrom were renting part of the building for their garage. Several automobiles were destroyed in the fire, but only one horse since the Olson Brothers had all their teams out in the woods.[4]

5. Fire destroyed the North Shore Garage, clothing store of J. T. Joynes and grocery store of J. C. Murphy. The Sterling Hotel was in extreme danger of catching fire. July 1925.[5] The J. T. Joynes store was located where the current Senior Center is now located.

6. The Steamer America struck a rock off Washington Harbor on Isle Royale, Michigan and sank on June 7, 1928.

7. Coast Guard Station was built in Grand Marais in fall of 1928.[6]

8. Chris Marken's Dry Goods Store on the east side of Broadway was razed by fire on February 1930.[7]

9. The Maple Hill Golf Course was opened in July 1935.[8]

10. Fire Razes Hicks' Store. The Trading Post on the west side and Grand Marais Bank on the east side of the store were saved. September 1936.[9]

11. Harold and Sherman Benson purchased the Midway Garage from L. P. Hirmer in the spring of 1946.[10]

12. The Sawtooth Mountain Ski Area opened on the hills north of Grand Marais in December 1948.[11]

13. Shold's Mobil Service Station, including International Harvester Agency, sold to Kenneth Lovass and Roger Shold on May 1, 1953.[12]

14. First train arrived at Taconite City in July 1953. It was a locomotive and observation car with company officials inspecting the project.[13]

15. In 1955, the Village of Grand Marais began construction of a water pipe into Lake Superior with a pump station on the shore next to the utilities building currently in the Tourist Park. The pipe was 20 inches in diameter and went out into the lake 300 feet. The water supply from the hills north of the town was no longer adequate. The new system was completed in the spring of 1956. [14]

16. A 30 x 100 foot addition to the south side of the high school gymnasium was finished in 1958 at a cost of $26,000.00.[15]

17. The new post office building on the northeast corner of Highway 61 and First Avenue West was dedicated in October 1959. Morris Quaife was the postmaster.[16] This is the current site of the Arrowhead Pharmacy.

18. Rafting of Pulpwood discontinued from Grand Marais and Sugar Loaf Landing by Consolidated Papers, Inc. at end of the 1972 season.[17]

19. In May 1973, Shold & Lovaas Service Station moved to southeast corner of Highway 61 and Broadway Avenue, the current location of Como Oil and Propane.[18]

(Endnotes)

1. *Cook County Herald*, June 6, 1903.

2. "Local History," Olga Soderberg, *Cook County News-Herald*, January 27, 1955, p. 2.

3. "The Fire Fiend," *Cook County Herald*, October 26, 1907, p. 5.

4. "Olson Brothers' Livery Barn Burns to Ground," *Cook County News-Herald*, January 28, 1920, p. 1.

5. "Three Business Houses Burned," *Cook County News-Herald*, July 16, 1925. p. 1.

6. "Nunstedt Gets Contract for Coast Guard," *Cook County News-Herald*, September 27, 1928, p. 1.

7. "Chris Marken's Store Razed by Fire Today," *Cook County News-Herald*, February6, 1930, p. 1.

8. "Golf Course is Ready for Use," *Cook County News-Herald*, July 25, 1935, p. 1.

9. "Fire Razes Hicks' Store. 100 Men Battle Blaze." *Cook County News- Herald*, September 10, 1936, p. 1.

10. "Midway Sold to Wisconsin Brothers," Cook County News-Herald, April 4, 1946, p. 1.

11. "Nelsons Open Ski Area; Ask Help in Housing Visiting Skiers," *Cook County News-Herald*, December 23, 1948, p. 1.

12. "Lovaas and Shold Buy Shold's Mobil Service," *Cook County News-Herald*, May 7, 1953, p. 1.

13. "First Train Reaches 'Taconite city'; Officials see Project Progress," 1/24/09*Cook County News-Herald*, July 9, 1953, p. 1.

14. "Work on Water Intake Project Suspended for Winter." *Cook County News-Herald*, October 27, 1955, p..

15. "What's New in Buildings?," *Cook County News-Herald*, November 12, 1958, p. 2.

16. "Post Office Building to Be Dedicated," *Cook County News-Herald*, October 20, 1959, p. 1.

17. "Consolidated Papers Will Discontinue Rafting of Pulpwood After '72 Season," *Cook County News-Herald*, July 22, 1971.

18. "Shold & Lovaas Station Will Move Next Week," *Cook County News-Herald*, April 26, 1973, p. 1.

Index